LIVE YOUR TRUTH AND LEAD

'At this important time in our evolution, as we awaken to new paradigms and new ways of being, Alexia offers us a gift. This book challenges us to explore and embrace the enduring, creative, fierce, intuitive and compassionate feminine power that resides within us all, and to allow that power to take root in our lives. Let this book illuminate your journey as you navigate a path of compassionate, heart-led activism in the world.'

Matt Hopwood
Author of *Mother: A Human Love Story*
and founder of A Human Love Story project

'For all the women in the world ... Live Your Truth and Lead reaches out to empower women to awaken their power within and play a leading role in the new challenges we face in times of climate crisis and social injustice. All of these challenges and missions need strong values, and, most of all, compassion – to love people and animals, all living. When women join their awoken energies together as sisters, change is possible. I found my strength with the EWMD Network. There, I felt that the souls met, and I smiled. I also felt the connectedness – that is when big things can happen.'

Claudia Schmitz
Founder and Director of Cenandu Learning Agency,
President (2008–09) of the European Women's Management
Development International Network, www.ewmd.org

'This phenomenal and well-researched book is very relevant to our time. It offers the reader an opportunity to invest in personal self-development, drawing from many traditions and sources, including philosophy, spiritual practice, and scientific research and analysis. It brings these strands together to underpin the theme of self-empowerment from a heart-centred, divine-feminine perspective. Its wisdom, however, is that it is not just a book for women but for every human being, and not just a manual for leadership but a guide for life.'

Jo Smith
Author of *The Adventures of Sydney Opera*,
a children's book about life values

DR ALEXIA MARY TZORTZAKI

LIVE YOUR TRUTH AND LEAD

EMPOWERING WOMEN TO BECOME
COMPASSIONATE LEADERS:
A PRACTICAL GUIDE

Copyright © 2024, Alexia Mary Tzortzaki.

All rights reserved. No part of this publication may be stored in a retrieval system, transmitted, reproduced, transcribed or translated into any language, in any form, by any means without the prior agreement and written permission of the author. Email: amtzortzaki@yahoo.gr

To order more copies of this title you can visit www.artofjoy.gr (the English version) or contact the author at the email above.

Originally the book was used as a textbook for the students and staff, participants of the workshop 'Empowering Women to Become Compassionate Leaders', held at Amrita University (Amrita Vishwa Vidyapeetham) in India and delivered by Dr. Alexia Mary Tzortzaki, in the Summer 2019.

Production Manager and Editor: Paul Baillie-Lane
Proofreading: Jo Smith
Cover design: Chris West
Publisher: Alexia Mary Tzortzaki, Sunflower Publishing

ISBN: 978-618-87086-1-7

1st edition

In honour of the woman 'behind' my ancestor, Kapetan Tzortzo-Michailos (Captain Michalis), who, when the time came (1866–97), was left with no choice but to support her husband in going into battle to defend the values of the Greek people, freedom and the magnanimity of spirit.

It is said that her name was Maria, but this has not been confirmed to date.

CONTENTS

Preface	xiii
Introduction	xv
CHAPTER 1: LEADERSHIP REDEFINED	**1**
The Golden Dawn of Compassionate Leadership	1
The Mandala of Compassionate Leadership	6
Self-Exploration	8
Self-Influence Towards Authenticity	10
Systemic Awareness	11
Relational Influence Towards Resonance	12
Self-Compassion	13
Mindfulness	14
Masculine and Feminine Energy	15
The Journey of an Empowered Woman	23
References and Further Reading	26
CHAPTER 2: YOUR THOUGHTS, YOUR REALITY	**29**
Universal Truths	29
The Garden of your Mind	36

The Conscious and the Unconscious mind	40
Values	44
Beliefs	55
Phobias and Fear	62
Thoughts	67
Your Reality and the Power of a Vision	78
References and Further Reading	83
CHAPTER 3: YOUR TRUTH, YOUR WISDOM	**85**
Self-Compassion – The Missing Link to Self-Leadership	85
Compassion and Over-Caring	87
Ego, Awareness and Humility	91
Self-Forgiveness	93
Self-Compassion	99
Time Management – How to be Stress-Free	105
Our Sacred Body – Allowing it to Flourish	118
Your Wisdom - Building Trust in YOU	135
Connect with Mother Earth – Space and Silence	135
The Maternal Line and our Intuition	139
Confidence	145
Hope – Trust – Faith	148
References and Further Reading	151
CHAPTER 4: YOUR HEART, YOUR VOICE	**153**
The Power of our Words	153
Heart Language	157

The Art of Active Listening	165
Resonance	167
Powerful Presence	171
Presenting in an Empowered Way	176
References and Further Reading	183
CHAPTER 5: LEAD BY EXAMPLE	**185**
Learning How to Die While You Are Still Alive	188
The Day-by-Day Intentions of a Heart-Led Leader	193
An Open Invitation to Join Forces	202
References and Further Reading	205
Acknowledgments	209
About Alexia	213

'Our deepest fear is not that
we are inadequate.

Our deepest fear is that
we are powerful beyond measure.

It is our light,
not our darkness,
that most frightens us.

Your playing small does not serve the world.

There is nothing enlightened about shrinking so that other people won't feel insecure around you.

And as we let our own lights shine,
we unconsciously give other people permission to do the same.

As we are liberated from our own fear, our presence automatically liberates others.'

Marianne Williamson

Your legacy is every life
that you have touched.

Maya Angelou

PREFACE

'Unshakable Hope' is the young woman's name, and she is a donation and original work of a bright young man, Giorgos Kontogiannos, from Rhodes, Greece. Originally, it was going to be on the front cover in colour, but the publication schedule was too short to allow time for this. The sketch was inspired by the ideas of my female friends whose opinion I sought. I wished for an image that would 'speak' to all women, irrespective of origin, religion or cast, and show their awakening, courage and freedom from their own limiting beliefs. They all unanimously agreed that we find such a reflection in Mother Nature, who symbolises the rising motion of the compassionate, feminine power.

Then my friend, Jo Smith, brought to my attention the 'tree hugging', or 'Chipko' (meaning 'to hug'), movement, originally led by Amrita Devi and 363 Bishnoi women and their families, who back in 1730 sacrificed their lives to save Khejadi trees. Similar movements have taken place since then in India, with 'Chipko' women protecting trees from logging in Northern Uttar Pradesh in 1974. And then again recently, in the district of Jharkhand, with Jamuna Tudu leading sixty courageous women to protect trees from the forest mafia and poachers.

The scene in the sketch takes place during 'Golden Dawn', while the sun has almost risen. The woman is, however, self-luminous. Her draped garment carries influences of the 'Karyatides', the elegant, sculpted female figures serving as architectural support columns to the ancient Greek temple of Artemis, situated on the Acropolis in Athens. A pigeon flies out of the woman's heart, signifying the 'silent' yet authentic and powerful language of compassion. The heroic lady's name, 'Unshakable Hope', is a reflection of a 'Golden Dawn' philosophy of life. A philosophy that carries the energy of the active power of hope. Remaining true to the vision. Not wishing for something to be better or passively hoping that someone else will come and save the day, but courageously and steadily walking the path of action and knowing deep inside that, despite appearances, light shall prevail.

The Sun will sure rise and it will be a Golden Dawn – not a cloud in the sky!

INTRODUCTION

The message that runs throughout this book is that self-compassion is the basis of self-leadership and the root of compassionate leadership. It aims to inspire women to find the courage to follow their dreams and learn how to dynamically influence top-level decisions by offering a more feminine response to a world in flames.

A selection of short tales, anecdotes and aphorisms, together with a rich collection of exercises and daily practices, validate you to 'Live Your Truth and Lead', offering guidance and practical pathways for women to:

- Connect with their inner core, wherein lies the field of infinite possibilities.
- Nurture their body-mind-soul coherence and balance their feminine/masculine energies in order to release their untapped creative powers.
- Discover their own life-enhancing values, serving as their compass to lead a life in flow, and as the 'fire' that incubates their dreams and visions.
- Elucidate and become free of their disempowering beliefs and fears.
- Learn to trust their wisdom, voice their truth with graceful sovereignty, and then actively live it.

Live Your Truth and Lead is an offspring of my life's vision, for which I had a calling in 2009. The calling is linked to education in the wider sense of the word, as reflected in the Greek word Παιδεία (*Pe-dia,* emphasis on the last syllabus*)*, which means to equip young people with life skills and to instill in them values that will nurture them to grow into self-reliant adults and virtuous, active citizens who care about their community and the Planet. This is an education that trains children and young people to become self-leaders, responsible for their own destiny, consciously and compassionately engaged with those around them. I believe that self-leadership is the key to developing the courage we need to follow our dreams. When we live out our dreams, we live a purposeful, meaningful, enriching life and this is when our eyes sparkle. Although rare, I'm sure you have seen such eyes. Wouldn't our world be a different, magical place if we all went around with sparkling eyes? I believe so!

My life's purpose is therefore to create an experiential 'School for Young Leaders', which will be a virtual and global space where young people can playfully and safely experiment and explore who they are and discover their unique talents. The insights and learnings will come through a series of tailor-made, out-of-class experiences, mostly in nature. The outcome of this school will be to see 'Sparkles in Young People's Eyes.' This is how I have named my vision.

I mention 'Sparkles in Young People's Eyes' here because it is intrinsically connected with the purpose of the book and the pivotal role that women play as leaders and custodians of children and young people whose eyes sparkle. The way I see it is that the seed of self-confidence is planted by a child's first and most intimate caregiver – in most cases, the child's biological mother. Without wishing to detract from the importance of a father in a child's development, the first feedback about life and a reflection of the child's self comes from the mother. A mother who expresses her love freely, embraces the child often and has a positive, fearless outlook towards life, confident of what she stands for and who she is, will have a profoundly positive effect on the child's level of self-value. So, the role of the mother is key for young adults to be confident and compassionate.

And yet, I would often ask myself: how does a mother, or any human being for that matter, consciously radiate loving-kindness under all circumstances? What is her constant source of energy? Reaching this level of unconditional love has been a continuing quest for me personally. As the saying goes, 'One of the best ways to learn something you do not know is to teach it.' So, after seven years of teaching a self-designed, self-leadership course to students in a provincial university on the island of Crete, Greece, I have come to appreciate that the constant source of energy is within us. And the only way we can access it is by focusing our gaze inwards, as we return to our core and begin to unveil our true, authentic self – the self that has direct connection to the divine.

The joy we experience from rediscovering our true self then generates the abundance of energy needed to serve others unconditionally. On such a path, we learn how to forgive and show compassion towards ourselves, how to receive and recognize our value, just like a mother would for her child. By first becoming a mother to ourselves, we allow our true potential to flourish, and offer the world the most precious gift: our own unique talent. As spiritual teacher Anita Moorjani said beautifully: 'Humanity's tapestry will never be complete without the full expression of our own unique thread.'

The conception of this book came with the opportunity I was offered by Amrita University in Kerala, India, to hold workshops for 'Empowering Women to Become Compassionate Leaders'. It also reflects my own transformative journey towards choosing to live my truth, especially those of my two most recent adventures. These began at the 'tender' age of fifty-one when after a fifteen-year long tenure, I resigned from my permanent and prestigious post at the University in Crete. I was becoming physically ill by increasingly toxic relationships both in work and with members of my close family. After filing a lawsuit against the university and much to the bewilderment of those around me, I adopted a minimalistic stance, sold my house and belongings, and embarked on a year-long road trip across Covid-stricken Europe. My companion was Libby (Liberty), my car that drove me to freedom. Unbeknown to me at the time, this journey became much more of an exploration of the most hidden corners of my psyche, rather than a sight-seeing trip across a geographical area. Upon my arrival in the UK, I did some volunteer work, and then various synchronicities brought me back to the place I was born: Wales. There, I continued my academic career as a human behaviour researcher and lecturer at Cardiff Metropolitan University. At the time, I thought Wales would be my home for a while and my new university would be a place where I could find like-minded co-creators.

The psyche, however, will not let you rest until you fulfil your purpose. So, two years later, a trip to the US to present an academic paper on 'the importance of purpose alignment and work life fulfillment', ironically, became the trigger for me to reinvent my life once again. I found myself standing at a crowd-packed, ultra-bright, neon New York Times Square right on the strike of midnight. It was mid-August 2023, not New Year's Eve, and the people looked like sleep-walking zombies unconsciously bumping into each other. This is when I got one of those eureka moments. In my eyes, the scene was symbolic of supreme materialism and a demonstration that we humans are completely missing the point of life.

Following my North Star, I now find myself returning to Crete as a transformed and even more passionate Light Worker, serving humanity and the planet. I am determined to devote my energy into writing, giving talks and expanding my HR training and coaching business, and be an outspoken advocate of a more inclusive, compassionate leadership paradigm. My ultimate aim is to continue collaborating with like-minded people and launch the 'School for Young Leaders'. I passionately believe such a space is needed more than ever before, especially now with the speedy advent of Generative AI and the danger of dehumanising our existence.

These two adventures have forced me to take a leap of faith and walk towards a more fluid, freer existence that is based on 'being in the now' rather than on constantly 'planning the next step'. I hope this fluidity comes through to you as you read the next chapters.

Just before writing this book, I was gifted another book by my parents where I came across such fluidity and graceful existence with the example of the women of the Minoan civilisation in Crete. The photographs of the 4,000-year-old excavated murals showed the magnificence of the Minoan ladies, who were certainly not housebound. Their society respected them for their wisdom and gave them the highest of privileges. Also, my discovery of the teachings of Amma, one of the few female spiritual leaders of our time, and reading the book by Swami Amritaswarupananda, *The Colour of the Rainbow*, about her unique leadership style and prolific humanitarian work, confirmed to me that compassionate female leadership is possible, and that many more women leaders are urgently needed to bring peace and harmony to our suffering world.

> **'We are all toffees.
> It is just our wrappings that are different.'**
>
> Amma

I believe that every one of us has a precious talent and that we are all unique. Every life has meaning and a significant purpose. We are here on Earth to learn from our experiences, serve others and to have fun while doing so! I believe in the power of thought. 'Thought creates matter and therefore our reality.' We are capable of inviting love, health, abundance and happiness into our lives. I'm not a supporter of any particular religion, sect or political party. Nevertheless, I do believe that we are made of energy and that we are much more than our tangible bodies. Being brought up as a Christian, I may slip into using the word 'God' out of habit. Over the years, I have developed a different understanding of the word, and I no longer mean a specific entity or the white-bearded man that watches us from Heaven.

Over the years, I have come to believe that 'God' is the divine that is present everywhere and *especially* inside of us. It is what others call 'Consciousness'. It is the 'here', the 'now'. 'Heaven' is for me the emptiness, the stillness, the space that I feel when I connect with nature, or when I gaze deep into the eyes of another person, or when I get absorbed by the smile of a stranger. This amazing, loving divine intelligence that we can experience anytime during our day is creator and guardian of the order of the cosmos. It is the Big Picture that we miss when we concentrate on chaotic, distressing circumstances.

These above are all core beliefs that guide me in my life as well as here, in my writing. Remaining focused on the Big Picture I have freely taken consultation from a diverse bank of knowledge, irrelevant of origin, so be prepared to remain open-minded.

'God dwells within you, as you.'

Elizabeth Gilbert

I have also reached the conclusion that all of the great sages and teachers have come to transmit the same message, that of unconditional love and unity. Under this premise, you will hopefully not be surprised to come across references to a wide variety of authors and teachers from right across the planet. As a result, a large spectrum of disciplines have been covered and intermingled in this work, such as psychology, psychophysiology, neuroscience and neuro-linguistic programming (NLP), sociology, biology, quantum physics, Christianity, Hinduism, ancient Greek philosophy, Buddhism, as well as educational theory and management and leadership research. An outspoken Greek academic Byzantinologist and the first female rector of Paris' Sorbonne University, Helene Glykatzi-Ahrweiler, once said that it is when one discipline shines a light on the other that new ideas and worldviews are born. So, I will ask you to keep an open mind at all times, as you come across wisdom from sources other than the ones you are accustomed to. As Amma tastefully says: 'We are all toffees. It is just our wrappings that are different.'

Please also bear in mind that, even though I have tried to write in a non-biased way, I'm human after all and have been conditioned like all of us by my cultural background and past experiences.

Moreover, as much as I will attempt to keep a high standard of academic and scientific accuracy, I will often introduce an undercurrent of playfulness and directness, since Παιδεία (*Pai-dia*, which means to equip young people with life skills and to instill in them values that will nurture them into becoming virtuous citizens*)* is rooted in the ancient Greek word παῖς *(pes)*, which means 'child'. In my experience, we learn better when we have fun. Part of the fun will also be for you to further explore the suggestions and ideas included in the book on your own. Therefore, an attitude of curiosity and discovery is necessary, and certainly is a leadership trait that allows you to remain fresh.

There are five chapters in this book. Chapters Two and Three are more expansive than the rest as I consider the topics they address to be the founding blocks for empowering women to become compassionate leaders. Once we establish a resonant connection with ourselves and develop self-love and self-care, we become our self's best friend. That is when we start knowing ourselves for the very first time and truly see our inner beauty. More importantly, however, we begin having trust and faith in ourselves. In this way, we will be a little less hungry for praise, acceptance and love. We will stop comparing ourselves to others and we will be able to say 'no' to unworthy requests or toxic people. Our thinking will become decidedly more authentic. Authentic thinking will be preceded by authentic action. As we think, we do. The repetition of authentic doing will become a behaviour, a way of life. Living authentically is living our truth. So, when we believe in our truth, we think our truth and we live our truth. And that is when our voice will be most heard!

On a more practical tone, you may need to equip yourself with a beautiful pen and notebook, so that you have enough space to complete the exercises suggested in this book, and also to take extra notes or jot down some of your thoughts. In fact, when you see the following symbol of a lotus flower in the book, it is a suggestion for you to take some time to contemplate the point being made before continuing to read on.

As a final note, this work has been infused with my love for humans and my soul's calling to see sparkles in young people's eyes. And what better way to make this manifest than by first seeing the sparkles in the eyes of their young mothers-to-be! May it be so. Γένοιτο!

CHAPTER 1

Leadership Redefined

The Golden Dawn of Compassionate Leadership

The Greek word for leadership is Ηγεσία *(pronounced: ige-sia, emphasis on the last syllabus)*, which comes from the ancient Greek word άγω *(pronounced: ago, emphasis on the 'a')*, meaning 'to guide'. So, for me, anyone who intentionally guides other people through their virtuous actions towards a vision of a better world is a leader. A mother who encourages her children to grow into being independent, caring adults is a leader; so is a microbiologist with a life-long passion to explore the humble human gut; so is a politician who dares to cry in public; so is a sculptress that is the only female that takes up the twenty-day challenge of carving a full-size marble statue of Peace in an open air yard in temperatures of 43° C; and so is a teacher who defies the prescribed syllabus and teaches children life skills by letting them run the classroom. A leader is also someone who knows of the high probability of a second tsunami wave hitting the shores and, despite this, courageously dives in the muddy waters to save lives. True leaders may have no title and they are not necessarily famous. Their daily practice is an expression of their authentic self, and it is their higher self and connection to the divine which constantly guides them. You can recognize a leader by the warming imprint he or she leaves on your heart after only one gaze and a radiating smile. All you have to do is notice the people around you carefully.

> **You can recognize a leader by the warming imprint he or she leaves on your heart after only one gaze and a radiating smile.**

Because we are sentient beings and we sense more than we listen in the content of language, it is the 'heart to heart' engagement that makes the difference. But where does compassion come into leadership, why are we discussing female leaders, and why now? We could start by stating the obvious: the economic argument. Well-established research centres, such as the HeartMath Institute, often publish findings which prove that organisations with compassionate *servant* leaders have happier, higher achieving people working in their teams. These are leaders that encourage the virtuous attitudes of authenticity, mutual trust and understanding, and promote self-led, autonomous working methods. The acceleration of the digital 'wave' due to Covid-19 has increased the skills gap between supply and demand. As an employer, it is not easy to find higher education graduates that are flexible, resilient and that demonstrate the high degree of interpersonal skills required for hybrid workplace environments. I think you will have noticed that this seems to be a worldwide phenomenon.

However, I would not like to focus only on the business case argument for compassionate leadership. We are at the early stages of a huge shift in the evolution of humanity, which is moving us from the centuries-old limiting belief that, in order to survive, each one of us needs to be in competition and engage in conflict with the rest, to the new belief that, in order *for all of us* to thrive, we need to cooperate with, help and care for each other.

The driving force in curtailing the spread of the Covid-19 virus were undoubtedly the frontline medical doctors and nurses who often had to take courageous on-the-spot decisions without having the time to consult anyone further up in the hierarchy. Their compassionate, servant leadership behaviours reminded us of the sensitive yet strong side of our human nature.

> **'Our inherent sensitivity is not a liability, it's a strength.'**
>
> Anita Moorjani

As with all paradigm shifts, the transition is not a bed of roses. Compassion is linked with love, so there are many old beliefs and myths about compassionate leadership to dissolve. A compassionate leader is still seen by the status quo as being too soft in times of consensus, or seemingly the one who shies away from tough conversations, or is overpowered by those who are more ruthless and loses control.

Sustainability and the thriving of the human race depend on an education system which, within young people, cultivates competencies that empower them for life, and those which computers cannot possess. The challenges posed by the Fourth Industrial Revolution – the need for flexibility and resilience, and the increasing lack of interpersonal skills in young adults – has led to a mismatch in the current higher education syllabi and employers' demands. Highly volatile and complex environments, the inevitable merging of cultures, the lack of privacy and the noticeable imbalance of natural resources, all lead to a rising climate of antagonism, conflict, war and division. In my view, our last chance for thriving as a human race cannot but lie in an education system which nurtures hearts, and much less minds, one that propagates virtues like honesty, kindness, generosity and connectivity, instead of only dry, cognitive knowledge and digital skills. That is, a system which encourages the development of self-leadership and ethical work principles, underpinned by a higher, intrinsic intent for civic engagement and a contribution to humanity.

> **'Our last chance for thriving as a human race cannot but lie in an education that nurtures hearts, and much less minds.'**

As I mentioned earlier, the ancient Greek language has a specific word for this philosophy of education: Παιδεία (*Pe-dia*). And the following African proverb captures the essence of the transformative power of *Pe-dia*, especially for girls and young women: 'When you educate a girl, you educate a whole community, whereas when you educate a boy, you only educate an individual.' In other words, when you empower a girl with education, you're not just impacting her life; you're influencing the entire community around her. Girls, when given the opportunity to learn and grow, often become catalysts for positive change, breaking the cycle of poverty and contributing to the well-being of their families and communities.

It is therefore more imperative than ever before that young women are given the opportunity to receive Pe-dia and encouraged to speak their truth and lead. Due to their ability to create life and their innate ability to collaborate and communicate with others in a compassionate and encouraging way, women are well suited for modern-day leadership roles. The question is, what is the road map for the development of a compassionate leader, and how can women be encouraged to acknowledge and decide that they already have all the power they need to take on leading roles? This book aims to illuminate such a way.

'Compassion is empathy with positive action.'
Dalai Lama

I have found that the best approach to learning something is through experience and then sharing with others in an interactive way, so you enrich this experience with collective wisdom. I guess this is why my soul decided to land in this lifetime as a woman in a highly patriarchal society and equally male-oriented religion (Greek Orthodoxy). I also used to think that it was only by coincidence that, although I often kept changing jobs, I still could not escape my fate of working in heavily masculine, testosterone-driven environments. Even in my romantic relationships, I seemed to attract men who were autocratic and domineering. I now know that all these circumstances rendered themselves as steps in my life's journey, and I'm grateful for the experience. I now also recognise that one of the main lessons I needed to learn before my departure is how to balance the male and female energies I have within me, and to return home to my authentic self, to become self-empowered and dare to show my true, beautiful colours under the blaring, Golden Dawn sun.

The Mandala of Compassionate Leadership

On the road to rediscovering who I am, and through the feedback of a self-leadership course I ran at the Hellenic Mediterranean University for seven years, I had an inspiration! When you fly by airplane, they give you safety instructions. What do the flight attendants say about the mask? 'In the case of an unlikely event, please first place the mask over your face, before helping others next to you to do the same.' This is code language for: 'In the unlikely event that we are going down and you need oxygen, please make sure that *you* are breathing well first before you help others next to you breathe!'

Is it not, therefore, the same for everything else we offer other people? How can you possibly show compassion, or give unconditional love to others, without first showing compassion and feeling this love and respect for yourself? Doesn't your cup of tea need to remain full if you are to keep sharing it with others?

And this is how the HEART-led™ framework for compassionate leadership was born.

The HEART-led™ model of compassionate leadership.

It stands on two premises:
1. To be a good leader, you first need to be able to lead yourself and be your own guide.
2. To be a compassionate, servant leader, you need to first know how to cultivate compassion towards yourself.

The HEART-led™ model suggests that, for a leader to be compassionate, they need to develop and work towards mastering four interlinking competencies: self-exploration, self-influence towards authenticity, systemic awareness and relational influence towards resonance. All four elements of the model are living, breathing, organic, co-dependent entities which, besides being milestones to work towards, also suggest what the path might be. The centre is the *alaya* ('abode' in Sanskrit) of the leader's heart. Unlike other leadership models, the linchpin of HEART-led™ is self-compassion, and it is a necessary approach, especially when you start exploring who you really are.

Though I respect the sacredness of a mandala, I cannot help but notice that the HEART-led™ model could suitably be transformed into one. If, for example, the dot in the middle was in the shape of a heart, then the middle area becomes the shape of a heart. The four gates correspond to the four competencies which need to be practiced to enter the realm of possibility of growing into a compassionate leader. The all-pervading and ever-present 'mindfulness attitude' of a leader takes its place on the circumference of the HEART-led™ mandala.

Even though the HEART-led™ model is the foundation of this book, I prefer not to follow a linear approach in uncovering its secret formula. This is because none of its elements can exist without the others, and each of the paths to achieve a high degree of competency in these often intermingles. I therefore feel that, for me to better serve as your guide on these paths, a more feminine, circular approach, such as the mandala, may be more appropriate. I will, however, make one exception here to briefly dissect and define the model's parts, so that we both share a similar perception of what I mean when I use the following terms.

Self-Exploration

Self-exploration is always where the journey starts and ends in order to sustain a compassionate leadership mindset. In other words, because the world around us keeps changing, and so do we, the ultimate goal of 'Know thyself', as suggested by the Ancient Greek philosophers, remains at a constant distance from us. So, if we say that our true self (*Atma* in Sanskrit) stands in the core of an upward spiral (see image below) and that we orbit around the core in an elliptical rather than a circular fashion, then there are times when we get very close to our core (point B) and, at other times, our distance increases (point A). No matter how well we think we know ourselves, there will always be beliefs and memories that are well tucked under the shadow of our unconscious. These can more easily be uncovered, as you will discover further on in this book, in a deeply relaxed and connected state of consciousness. The good news is that, as we evolve spiritually, the overall distance from our true self gets smaller because we are higher up the spiral and closer to its core.

Upward spiral of evolution (the rod in the middle represents our true self).

Our key life values are closely related to our life purpose and the unique talents that we are here to actively place in the service of humanity and the planet. The need to identify our key life values is not coloured by a romanticised view of our existence and not in line with an altruistic, servant mindset. It echoes the urgent need to address our existential needs, and those of all other future leaders, entrepreneurs and the workforce, and is the most effective way to unlock valuable untapped potential. Being more conscious of their values and unique talents will empower school leavers to make more purpose-aligned educational choices; educational establishments to provide more meaningful learning interventions, and enterprises to leverage their human resource capital more sustainably and agilely. Such syncing will contribute to thriving economies and reduced mental health issues.

Our key life values are closely related to our life purpose and the unique talents that we are here to actively place in the service of humanity and the planet. The need to identify our key life values, is in my view, urgent and an issue linked to our overall sustainability. I see life values as an echo of the existential needs of leaders, entrepreneurs and the workforce. Knowing our life values and allowing them to guide us in our actions is an effective way to unlock our society's untapped potential. For instance, when school leavers are more conscious of their values and unique talents they will be more empowered to make purpose-aligned, life-enriching educational choices. In response to this, educational establishments will be called to provide more meaningful learning interventions, and organisations will be aligned to leverage their human resource capital more sustainably and agilely. Such syncing will contribute to thriving economies and reduced mental health issues.

When uncovered, disempowering beliefs in particular need a gentle, kind attitude towards our self. The hardest part for me with this kind of belief was forgiving myself for remaining stuck in it for so many years. The art of self-forgiveness is at the root of self-compassion, and its practice is also explained in this book. As you will discover in the next chapter, disempowering beliefs are a negatively charged force and can be an obstacle to realizing your dreams. So, developing the competency of continuous self-exploration can be as simple as finding out what food makes you feel well and which does not, or as complicated as discovering at what point in your life you decided that you were not of any value.

Self-Influence Towards Authenticity

It takes a huge amount of courage to live a truly authentic, amplified existence. As Elizabeth Gilbert mentions in *Big Magic*, to hunt inside yourself in order to uncover your hidden treasures is what separates a mundane existence from a more enchanted one. The mundane existence is similar to the archetype of a soldier and the enchanted existence closer to the archetype of a warrior. A warrior lives a dignified, honorable life and is blatantly honest, even when this will mean losing a few fans, as opposed to a soldier who enters into every single battle to save face, who enjoys flattery and is afraid of disapproval. The influencing drive towards authenticity, besides enthusiastic self-exploration, requires amongst other qualities humility, resilience, clear seeing and a large dose of curiosity. It also requires absolute awareness and openness (śūnyata in Sanskrit, meaning 'void') to what comes next in life, and openness towards others.

A true leader allows their raw heart to be exposed to the world, to be vulnerable. When you stand as your authentic self, it is such a relief! Have you ever tried to take this stance yourself? This is something I learned from one of my teachers, Chögyam Trungpa Rinpoche. He was always very open about his private life with his students. When I first started teaching and had not yet come across this attitude, I was very 'stuck up' and fixated on my reference point of being a professor. It was so uncomfortable, and even the clothes and high heels I wore hours on end to fit the part were tormenting me. Then I came across the idea of simply being myself, which I gradually cultivated, and now I quite enjoy the feedback and crystalline advice I get from my young students about my private affairs. The biggest gift of all is, however, the heightened connectedness that I receive when standing in front of my classroom 'naked'.

Systemic Awareness

This is about being constantly aware not only of your micro-cosmos but also of your macro-cosmos. It is a state only achieved by maintaining presence. It is about being in 'the NOW state', as my NLP instructor Terry calls it – not in the future, nor in the past. This state allows you to be aware of what is going on inside you, and also externally. Although I intend to cover this topic extensively in one of the following chapters, as it is pivotal to leading with compassion, I would like to add that being present, as far as the outside world is concerned, informs you of changes in the pulse of the world. It highlights patterns that are about to emerge and new ones that evolve from old ones, helping you to be better prepared of uncertainty. Systemic awareness helps you to reframe situations, form various future scenarios and expand on available options to face challenges. It is as if you have an eagle's view of the world, taking a panoramic photograph of what you see.

In developing the competence of systemic awareness, you realize that 'it's the difference that makes the difference'. You walk into a meeting room, and before you blurt out your need, you pick up on the air of annoyance which lingers in the room as a remainder of an argument that your colleagues have just had. This awareness helps you realize that this is not a good moment to ask for something. So, systemic awareness not only helps us be more discerning in our decision making but also provides useful feedback for us to actively create resonant relationships.

Relational Influence Towards Resonance

As extensively researched and scientifically proven in the international bestseller *Connected* by Nicholas Christakis and James Fowler, we humans are wired to connect. In other words, whether we use voice or actions, they have an effect on our environment. Famous for his studies of the water crystals that form in our bodies, Masaru Emoto has proven that even our thoughts send out vibrations and to extend this discovery. Our ability to connect through our electromagnetic properties were also proven through the HeartMath Institute's extensive research into heart rate variability (HRV). These scientists have produced scientific evidence that our heart has an intelligence of its own, and that we relate well to sentient beings around us when we have heart coherence. Heart coherence is about intentionally practicing creating *resonant relationships* with our external world. One very important ingredient for building rapport and nurturing healthy relationships, whether in work or our personal life, is to be grounded in the NOW. Mindfulness is therefore, as we will explore in the next chapters, yet again the starting point.

Also, in the area of relational influence, we will be looking into how to develop an enchanting presence without losing humility, the difference between expressing our needs in an assertive and in an aggressive way, the adoption of strategies for non-violent communication, how to be of help to others when they need us, and techniques for delivering an unforgettable presentation.

> **'Compassion is the language the blind can see and the deaf can hear.'**
>
> Amma

Self-Compassion

Even though I honestly *do* forget at times, I have started to seriously consider the idea that we are all basically good inside, that we all have a soft spot, as Chögyam Trungpa often used to say. This soft spot is *compassion*. Even a criminal has a soft spot, and even the worst bully in the world has a soft spot or else they would not fall in love. As Amma says, 'Compassion is the language the blind can see and the deaf can hear.'

Compassion needs to move one step further than empathy (i.e., feeling another's pain), and it has three aspects. Firstly, you need to cultivate the ability to step into another person's shoes and understand their pain on a cognitive level. Secondly, you need to momentarily feel their pain. And thirdly, and more importantly, you need to step out of their shoes in order to engage in the most suitable action to help ease their pain.

Self-compassion is, from my personal and teaching experience, the starting point for bringing out our inbuilt loving-kindness nature, our compassionate nature. This is the reason why self-compassion has been made the linchpin of the HEART-led compassionate leadership model. Research has shown that students that view their academic failures as opportunities to learn and not as shortcomings or as unfortunate events are more compassionate towards their peers. Managers that are self-compassionate and practice self-care are less prone to burnout, less drawn towards guilt trips, avoid defensive or aggressive behaviours, and are more open to diversity and innovative ideas.

Women especially, as we will see in the section on time management, are inclined to neglect their basic needs in order to take care of their families, and to validate themselves in their workplaces. When our energy reserves are close to zero, we get frustrated, tired and sick, and that is when our beautiful, unconditional love becomes a love with conditions.

We give love in order to receive something in return, maybe love itself. So, the premise here is that, unless our cup of tea is full, we cannot share our tea with others. When the mother in the family is sick, the whole family falls apart. She needs to be well and fulfilled. That is when all around her are happy. Self-compassion is a neglected area, not only from a religious point of view but also from an academic and educational perspective. We are not taught the value of self-compassion, as it is often conflated with egocentricity. Self-compassion is certainly a theme that will be running right throughout this book, offering practical ideas on how to nurture it.

Mindfulness

In the HEART-led model of compassionate leadership, you will note that mindfulness lies on the circumference of the circle. This is because a mindful attitude needs to permeate all the thoughts, emotions and actions of a compassionate leader. But what is mindfulness and what does it mean to be mindful? I would not have been able to value its necessity in my life if I had not spent time in retreats with Shambhala, a Buddhist organisation, where I learned in a very experiential way what it means to sit on the ground and follow your breath, and then appreciate the magical transformation that takes place in your life as a result. Even though mindfulness originates from the East, it is now widely used worldwide as a tool in therapy for all kinds of neuroses and ailments, such as panic attacks, stress and pain control.

Thich Nhat Hanh, the famous Vietnamese monk and teacher, explains beautifully in his book *Mindful Movements*: 'Mindfulness is our ability to be aware of what is going on both inside of us and around us. It is the continuous awareness of our bodies, emotions and thoughts. Through mindfulness, we avoid harming ourselves and others, and can work wonders.' For me personally, mindfulness has nothing to do with religion, but has a great deal to do with my spiritual evolution. I have discovered that it is the gateway to communicating with my true, higher self. It takes me to my inner core, where my heart resides. It takes me back home (*alaya*). Meditation is only one way to train yourself in being mindful. It is, however, a very powerful tool to achieve this goal. A variety of mindfulness and meditation exercises will be provided in this book. As a taster, here is a little practice that you can easily do anytime during your day:

PRACTICE #1
Mindfulness – Changing labels

Wherever you may be sitting, take a careful look around you and focus on every single object that grabs your attention. Give the object a label other than the label it normally has. For instance, you look at a chair and you call out 'frying pan'. For a greater effect, do this while moving in the room and call out the object's newly assigned label while simultaneously pointing at the object. Then speedily move on to the next object in the room and give it a new label. Repeat this process for about five minutes.

This is an excellent grounding exercise, and it is guaranteed to bring you back to the present moment.

'The present moment is the only moment we can actually experience and influence.'

Thich Nhat Hanh

Mindfulness is certainly a concept that can be extensively discussed and analyzed, but this sort of activity is all to do with our cognition. It is all theory! The question that might often arise is, 'How mindful are you, and how will you know when you are?' Mindfulness can only be internalized when practiced and experienced.

EXERCISE #1
Self-exploration – How mindful are you?

This is a quick self-check of your average experience of the following situations in your daily life. Place the corresponding number next to each question:

1 = never, 2 = seldom; 3 = sometimes, 4 = most times, 5 = always.

Try to complete the test within one minute.

- When people introduce themselves to me, I have difficulty in recalling their name if I need to speak to them again, even when this is shortly after.

- I find it hard to remember what food I ate the day before yesterday.
- I walk or drive somewhere in a rush, without noticing people's faces along the way, or nature.
- I realise my body is in pain only after it becomes unbearable.
- I often bump into furniture and accidentally drop objects.

The lower your total score, the more mindful and connected to life you are. So, the lowest score of five corresponds to a very high level of mindfulness, and the highest score of twenty-five corresponds to a very low level of mindfulness.

Bear in mind that your mindfulness levels may vary slightly from time to time, especially during highly distressing periods or periods of mental and bodily exhaustion. So, do not rush to judge yourself if your score was high. Simply observe, be gentle with YOU, and curious as to why this might be happening. Such an approach is often all that is needed to 'shift things' inside.

Masculine and Feminine Energy

The balance of masculine (*yang*) and feminine (*yin*) energies is a vast and sensitive issue for many of us. It is, however, important to address because the imbalance between *yang* and *yin* energies harbours serious consequences for our whole planet. These two energies are often confused with the two genders: male and female. I have often come across women who have a strong, masculine drive, and, likewise, men who have a softer, feminine nature. *Yang* and *yin* are two opposing forces that most cultures see as the cause of conflict, although when they coexist harmoniously, as in nature, they can become the source of our vital energy and happiness. Everything contains the seed of its opposite and both are interconnected: our out-breath and our in-breath, expansion and contraction, left hand, right hand, a straight line, a curved line, matter, anti-matter. Without darkness we could not recognise the existence of light.

'Everything contains the seed of its opposite and both are interconnected.'

But what does 'balance' really mean? During the 3rd century BC, the Greek philosopher Aristotle studied the idea of the 'middle ground' (μέτρον ἄριστον, *metron ariston*) in connection to a person living a virtuous, balanced life. The middle of two extreme characteristics was for him the 'middle ground', the one extreme being the exaggerated form of the characteristic and the other extreme being the minimal expression of the characteristic. 'Courage' would therefore be the middle ground for 'audacity', with 'cowardice' or 'prudence' the middle ground for 'indulgence' and 'complacency', and 'magnificence' the middle ground for 'sloppiness' and 'heartlessness'. As you can see, the middle ground (or balance) is relative to one's own subjective estimation since the characteristics are not measurable.

So, as with all opposites, and following Aristotle's analogy, balancing them out does not necessarily mean having 'equal amounts of each'. It simply means using the expression of each of the opposites in the appropriate 'volume', depending on the situation that arises. For instance, if a mother is in a situation where her ten-year-old son is insisting on her buying him a toy she cannot afford, she will do well to use her logic, be strict and firm with him (*yang* energy). If, however, the next day she is still following a strict attitude and lacks her usual softness and affection (*yin* energy), her behavior is no longer warranted and is out of context and balance. So, when we talk about the balance needed between masculine and feminine energies, it is important to note that it does not necessarily mean that equal amounts of these energies will bring this balance, but that there needs to be the right amount of both energies, depending on what is called for in any given situation. When the masculine and feminine principles of life merge in a balanced way, life expands and all of our relationships flourish.

This can be better understood if we examine the balance of *yin* and *yang* in our internal world. We are in a state of *yin* when we are resourceful and solve a problem creatively with original solutions, are flexible, go with the flow and don't fight a situation, express our feelings, accept the other as they are, when our life is in serious danger, when our intuition warns us that someone is lying to us, when we have lost the sense of time because we are engrossed in a beautiful piece of music, or when we console someone. Our father was in a *yin* state if, when we were little, he would secretly wink at us while our mum was telling us off.

We enter a state of *yang* when we need to organise a journey, express our wants and needs, go to a meeting with an agenda in mind, have to solve a mathematical equation using our analytical thinking, need to study an architectural design, need to set boundaries with others, or want to win a tennis match or get promoted at work. Our mother was in her *yang* state when she would check the cupboards and write down a shopping list.

For most of my adult years, I have been quite strategic in my thinking and in a *yang* state. Knowing this, during my recent year-long road trip across Europe, I purposefully took a 'leap of faith' and threw myself into more fluid, *yin* states. This allowed me to explore what it is like to *not* know exactly where I am headed or where I will sleep every night. It got me out of my comfort zone. This was very unfamiliar at times. Travelling and crossing country borders during the pandemic added to the stress I sometimes felt. Looking back, I do not regret any moment of this transitional journey. I now realise that this new way of being is possible, and that when we follow our heart, no real harm comes to us. In many respects, not planning each step allowed me to be freer. Being 'out of my mind' meant that I was more into my body. Besides helping me balance my masculine and feminine aspects, I became more resilient and less dependent on external reference points. My main reference point became my earthy, gut feeling – my own centre.

As I will explain in the last chapter, the organic approach to being a traveller revealed synchronicities and opportunities that would have been missed if I had a specific route plan. So, it may be an interesting experiment to notice how you react when you do some 'aimless wandering'. This means going out of your front door and simply allowing your body instead of your mind to take you for a walk, much like a dog on a lead would.

PRACTICE #2
Balancing masculinity and femininity within us

Whilst standing upright, open your hands wide. Then, slowly and in the shape of an embrace, bring them in front of you. Now, form with each hand an 'open tiger mouth' shape. Join the 'open tiger mouths' together diagonally so that they lock together in a firm handshake.

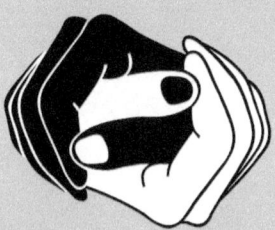

Notice how well they fit into each other, and then notice how, with a little imagination, they form the union of the well-known 'yin' and 'yang' circle – just like the circular sequence of night and day, darkness and light, softness and hardness, cusp and peak of a wave, the moon and the sun, water and fire, and also our own feminine and masculine energy within.

This exercise takes seconds to do, and you can repeat it as many times as you need during your day.

Another way of looking at the interconnectedness of the masculine and feminine energies is that the 'act of balancing' is just like balancing anything that is in pairs around us. Then when they balance, they cease to exist as two separate entities and are united into one. I'm sensing that that is where peace and space exist. That is where we can 'find' bliss: in unity. And if peace and bliss exist within us, then these qualities emanate to our outer world. 'As within, so without.' Our inner world is projected onto our outer world! By keeping the *yin* and *yang* energies in balance within us, we project this balance outwards to the people around us, in our family and our workplace. It all starts from us.

EXERCISE #2:
Self-exploration – masculine/feminine behaviors

Draw a 'T' shape on a blank page of your notebook and make two lists of what you think are masculine and feminine behaviors. It may be interesting to discuss this list with your friends and then contemplate how the heightened awareness of these two different energies inside you can improve the balance in your life by being more conscious of which of the two is mostly needed, depending on the situation that you are facing.

Then make a note of whether you use more of the one and less of the other, and, if so, how could you strive for a more balanced approach to life. For example, if you find yourself being a compulsive 'doer', maybe you need to

> find more ways to simply 'be'. Be more of a 'human being' instead of a 'human doing'.
> Or if, like me, you act hastily at times out of impatience, you can see if you can train yourself to be more patient and let time be your guide.

As one last tip, I often use high-quality essential oils to self-heal. Rose essential oil is known to stimulate the heart chakra, self-love and love towards others, and to aid the balancing of feminine and masculine energies within us. Growing roses in our garden also promotes this balance. So, let there be roses!

The Journey of an Empowered Woman: 'He for She' – Equal Partners

It was some 5,000 years ago when women were acknowledged for their gentle strength and, as conservers of culture, were seen as the main force which could maintain and bring peace and harmony. As I mentioned earlier, the 4,000-year-old murals of the Minoan women are living proof that females in those times were cherished and respected. During spiritual rituals, high priestesses stood right at the head of the processions. The more athletic of the women participated as equals to their male counterparts in a unique and extremely dangerous sporting event, where athletes performed acrobatics on the back of a raging bull. Minoan women are often depicted being carried in a special carriage. Their main god was Mother God, and she was often seen as the Earth Mother. The Minoan queen was admired as a goddess and as a woman who carried great wisdom.

Similar stories come from other civilisations, such as the story of Tara in Tibet. As Tara is a female goddess, it is acceptable for women to pretend to be Tara themselves; in other words, to act and talk in the same way that the goddess would and see the essence of Tara in each and every person they encounter. In the ancient Indian tradition, the husband would call his wife '*patni*', which in Sanskrit means 'life guide'.

In the very early civilisations of our world, women's bodies were viewed as a sacred temple and, at the time of their menses, they were allowed space to connect to their higher selves and were consulted by their fellow villagers on the most serious of matters. In later times, women have fought to win the right to vote, have fought for girls to have the right to an education, have fought to save trees, have fought to break the 'glass ceiling' within companies, rebelled against wearing the hijab and have accomplished many audacious acts, whether known or unknown. As co-founder of Rising Women, Rising World, Dr. Rama Mani says, 'Today, women are shaping transformations in unexpected, creative and beautiful ways, in every part of the globe, even in the most divided war zones and amidst excruciating crises.'

There is a memory of a society where the masculine and feminine principles of life co-existed and intermingled harmoniously. To become empowered as a woman, we might therefore be wise to call upon the collective intelligence of our deep ancestral programming and use it as the anchor to prevent us from drifting aimlessly in the ocean of the male/female duality. To become empowered, we do in fact already know what each one of us needs to do. Maybe we simply need to help each other remember the path to re-finding the power within.

In Carol Schaefer's book, *Grandmothers Counsel the World*, one of the thirteen elders, Flordemayo, a female Mayan elder from Nicaragua, advises young women to look at *themselves* for the answers to what they need, and not to expect their partners to cover these needs: 'Go back to yourself and see what you are going to do for yourself first. Balancing marriage, children, work, home and *self* is an incredible journey. Still, the only one you can really answer to is yourself.'

> **'The more you know about something, the better you can handle it. The more you know about Yourself, the better you can handle Yourself.'**
>
> Sadhguru, from his 'Mystic Quotes'

The HeForShe campaign launched by the UN in 2014 is closer to the idea of how I see the empowered woman's journey. The HeForShe Alliance is made up of global industry leaders and has the mission of engaging men and boys for a gender-equal world. It is about a joint partnership of men and women. In this season of radical role model remodeling, where the majority of women in power follow hierarchical patriarchal styles, not even women are quite sure what it is like to abide in a balanced masculine/feminine nature. Both men and women need to work individually and consciously towards balancing their own internal masculine/feminine energies. Self-awareness is required, as is a deep desire to explore every aspect of oneself for the sake of humanity. And, simultaneously, women need to keep continually inviting in the men in their lives in order to elevate their status to that of a man.

The HeForShe paradigm was exemplified by the Iranian football team at the 2022 FIFA World Cup when they declined to sing their national anthem before their match with England in support of the Mahsa Amini protestors. Many fans held up banners saying 'Woman, Life, Freedom'.

I believe it is a woman's task to find her way onto the path of living her truth. Then, from the grounded position of living it out, she can become more assertive and explicit in asking for help from men. And it is a man's task to become more active in listening and permitting his heart to be open and vulnerable. Both tasks require willpower and courage. Even small, family level acts of bravery create a butterfly effect of ripples and shifts in consciousness.

References and Further Reading

Amma (Sri Mata Amritanandamayi Devi), (2011), *Nectar of Wisdom*, Mata Amritanandamayi Mission Trust, Kerala, India.

Bradden, G. (2008), *The Spontaneous Healing of Belief*, Hay House Inc.,US.

Boulter, M., (2005), *Extinction: Evolution and the End of Man*, Columbia University Press, U.S.

Boyatzis, R. and McKee, A., (2005), *Resonant Leadership: Renewing Yourself and Connecting with Others Through Mindfulness, Hope and Compassion*, Harvard Business Review, US.

Brachio, A. (2020), 'Why is empathy crucial to the leadership imperative in the Covid-19 era?' LinkedIn [online] https://www.linkedin.com/pulse/why-empathy-crucial-leadership-imperative-covid-19-era-amy-brachio (Accessed on 11/03/2022)

Christakis, N. and Fowler, J., (2011), *Connected: The Surprising Power of Our Social Networks and How They Shape Our Lives*, Little, Brown Spark.

Chögyam Trungpa, (1984), *Shambhala: The Sacred Path of the Warrior*, Shambhala Publications, Inc., Boston, US.

De Zulueta, P. (2021) 'How do we sustain compassionate healthcare? Compassionate leadership in the time of the COVID-19 pandemic', *Clinics in Integrated Care*, Vol. 8, p.100071.

Enders, G. (2015), *The Gut*, Scribe Publications, UK.

Elston, T. (2019), *The NOW state®*, NLP World, UK.

Gilbert, E. (2015), *Big Magic*, Bloomsbury Publishing Plc., UK.

Hannam, D. (2018), Key Note speech at the *European Conference for Democratic Education* (EUDEC 2018), August 2018, Crete, Greece.

Kyriakaki-Sfakaki, A. (2015), *The Woman in Minoan Crete* (in Greek), Mystis Publishing Company.

Masaru, E., (2007), *The miracle of water*, Atria Paperback, NY.

Miyagawa, Y., Taniguchi, J. and Niiya, Y., (2018), 'Can self-compassion help people regulate unattained goals and emotional reactions toward setbacks?', *Personality and Individual Differences*, 134, pp.239-244.

Moorjani, A., (2021), Sensitive is the New Strong: The Power of Empaths in an Increasingly Harsh World, Yellow Kite Publishing, US.

Schaefer, C. (2006), *Grandmothers Counsel the World*, Trumpeter Books, Shambhala Publications.

Sharma, R. (2010), *The Leader Who Had No Title*, Free Press.

Swami Amritaswarupananda Puri, (2013), *Color of the Rainbow: Compassionate Leadership*, M.A. Center Publishers, India.

The Kings Fund, (2019), Five myths of compassionate leadership. The Kings

Fund. https://www.kingsfund.org.uk/blog/2019/05/five-myths-compassionate-leadership (Accessed 27/09/2022).

Tzortzaki, A.M. (2019), "The Need for Teaching Compassionate Self-Leadership in a University Setting", in *12th Annual Conference of the EuroMed Academy of Business proceedings of the International 2019 Conference*, Salonica, Greece.

Tzortzaki, A.M. (2022), Developing compassionate self-leadership: a conceptual framework for leadership effectiveness in the digital age, *Journal of Global Business Advancement*, vol. 15, no.3, pp. 272-296.

Tzortzaki, A.M. (2023), Workers of the future: Is aligning a self-led life to work purpose the solution to worker engagement?, *83rd Annual Meeting of the Academy of Management,* Boston, US, 4-8 August.

Tich Nhat Hanh, (2008), *Mindful Movements*, Parallax Press, CA, US.

CHAPTER 2

Your Thoughts, Your Reality

Universal Truths

Any great leader needs to be aware of certain 'truths' about our world so they can build up the courage to face life and ride gracefully over the waves. We are all a mirror image of the universe. We were created by the same laws that govern our micro- and macro-cosmos. By studying both ourselves and the universe, we can become more mindful about what steps we need to take in order to attain what we aim for, or how to behave in order to contribute towards building resonant relationships. In this section you will find some of what I know to be the most essential and universal truths.

Life is hard

The first 'truth' is that life is hard, and things will often happen that will make you feel that life is unfair. For example, you might have put in a lot of hard work in an assignment and then, when the marks are announced, the teacher congratulates one of your fellow students on their work, ignoring yours, whereas *you* know full well that they have plagiarised it. Or you have been married to someone for nine years and then find out that they have been having an affair for most of your married life. These are, of course, just some examples of life's unfair handouts. And then, you might ask yourself, 'Why me?' One good friend of mine, Sofia, once told me when I was complaining about my life: 'I think the best thing you can do for today is to visit the children's cancer hospital down the road from here. That should put things in perspective for you!'

Life is beautiful

The second universal truth is that life is also very beautiful, as long as you learn to 'get' the lesson every time something seemingly bad happens to you. There is always a lesson! It may come to you fifteen years down the line while you are having a shower or making your bed. Every cloud has its silver lining and every hardship prepares you and makes you stronger for your next step towards liberation from guilt and fear. The closer you get towards this liberation (the upward spiral), the more you notice how nature has endowed your surroundings with beauty and love. I often feel now that when I take big leaps in my life in search of my authentic self, there is always a protective net below the vast empty space that I leap into, so the risks I take are calculated by default. There is something there that wants me to succeed, that wants me to thrive!

The law of attraction

I'm sure you have often come across this law, but, like myself, often forget it when you are gripped by the fear of failure, or by the fear of your train being delayed and then missing a flight. As we will see in the sections that follow, modern-day physics (quantum physics) has proven that our thoughts are energy and that, if we think of something persistently, then this thought will materialise. In other words, *energy* will transform into *material*: 'As above, so below' or 'The inside is the outside.' The consequence of this for your understanding of how life works is a lot more serious than you may imagine. And this consequence is that only *you* are responsible for your happiness. Why? Because it all has to do with *how we react* towards what life throws at us and has nothing to do with *what* it throws at us. There is a great saying I like to remember: 'When life throws lemons at you, make lemonade.'

In space and silence lies the answer

This universal truth is related to the Law of Attraction. Haven't you noticed that if you chase after something, or someone, it/they will move further away from you? For instance, I was desperately trying to get transferred to another city while working at my university, and the more I chased after this idea, the worst my job situation became. Only when I dropped the case and relaxed did the transfer come through. In fact, the transfer took place in the most magical of ways, and definitely not in a way that I had foreseen. Letting go of your pull on a situation, an object or a person, and allowing for space and silence to come in, brings freshness and inspiration into your life, helping you, in this way, to 'attract' instead of 'chase' after the beauty of life. Chögyam Trungpa, a Buddhist teacher, used to say that inspiration comes in a flash of a second, just when the hand that holds your calligraphy pen is in mid-air and is about to land on the blank page.

All things change constantly

Contemplating the impermanent nature of our existence is an exercise I would highly recommend. Steve Jobs, the founder of Apple, mentioned in a graduation speech: 'Remembering that you are going to die is the best way I know to avoid the trap of thinking you have something to lose.' He also used a little daily trick question as a barometer to judge whether he was on track with what his heart wanted. 'If today were the last day of my life, would I want to do what I am about to do today?' And whenever the answer was 'no' for too many days in a row, he would know he needed to change something.

Additionally, on the issue of impermanence, consider how volatile your emotions are. Haven't you ever noticed that, if one day you are 'down' then the next day when something else happens you are flying up high as a kite? We feel insecure and out of control when we do not know what tomorrow brings. But haven't we got enough on our plates for today? In any case, things do not only change seemingly in an unfavorable way, but they also change in a way that may help us. We, as humans, especially when we are disconnected from our higher selves, are far too shortsighted to know what is good or what is bad for us, and we often take unsolicited advice from anyone that dishes it out. This is another reason why it is important to develop a sound relationship with our self, so that we develop the discretion and wisdom to make good decisions for our future, without being swayed left, right and centre by too many opinions.

EXERCISE #3
Self-exploration – Is it good or bad?

Contemplate three major decisions you have taken in the past and see how you feel about them now. Make a note for each one of them and consider these questions:

- Have you already seen some outcomes as a result of taking these decisions?
- Did you take theses decisions on your own?
- Did someone else decide for you or did you take someone's advice?
- If this was the case, looking back, was this the right person to give you this advice?

Whether you now think it was a good or bad decision, what lesson can you take during this self-exploration exercise about the nature of things and about your values now and your values in the past?

On a scale from 1-5 (1 = the least, 5 = the most), how much do you trust yourself to take important life decisions?

Note some examples of what these life decisions could be.

'In the end, all will go well. If they are not going well now, then it means that the end has not yet come!'

Wolf

The map is not the territory

This is a phrase coined by the scholar in semantics, Alfred Korzybski. In short, it means that our perception of reality is not reality itself. For instance: 'A piece of paper on which we have written "sugar" will not taste sweet' (Amma). Nor does your name, or my name, possibly capture the essence of who we both are. This universal truth has many implications in the way we view the world – on our level of adaptability and, more importantly, on how effective we are when we communicate with other people. Remembering this truth is a golden key to compassionate leadership. 'The map is not the territory' will be explored in detail in the sections that follow.

The law of cause and effect

This is a natural law and is not about punishment or reward. It follows nature's tendency towards balance. As you give, you will receive. Positive actions produce positive outcomes, and vice versa. The apparently simple logic of 'karma' is hard for most of us to put into practice in a positive way during our busy, daily lives. This is disregarding what most spiritual paths affirm about karma – that karma accumulated in this lifetime is carried through to the next lifetime.

This is very important to understand from a leadership perspective. I recently had a discussion with my daughter as to why it seems to be hard to motivate young people, at least here in Greece, to become interested in taking a more active role in protecting our planet, when it is *their* children that will suffer from the pollution in the years to come. She gave an interesting explanation. She said that sometimes we humans forget that we are not simply a black dot on a white page, with no connection with other 'dots'. When we feel like a 'black dot' on a white page, we feel helpless and weak. We tend to think that, no matter what individual action we take, even if it is as little as starting to recycle our plastic garbage or collect plastic bottle tops at home, this effort will have no bearing on such a huge planetary issue, and is futile. This attitude then transforms into apathy.

My daughter suggested that, to change such a mentality, we need to start 'connecting the dots'. By this, I believe she meant that we need to exercise our muscles of curiosity and observation: to start seeing life, and our actions, with the eyes of an eagle, from a much higher place. In this way, we will see the motifs that keep repeating in our *own* behavior first, and then in those of others. We will begin to realise the seeds of our habitual patterns are beliefs, and that these, in turn, are a result of our values. The significance of beliefs and values, and their exploration, will be the focus of the following section.

The law of the octave

Every new idea, new relationship and new project tends to follow the following eight steps of evolution, much like the musical octave:

1. Favourable circumstances (Do) – the 'soil' is fertile
2. Implantation (Re) – the 'seed' is planted
3. Insemination (Mi) – the 'seed' is inseminated
4. Birth (Fa) – the 'seed' starts opening
5. Development (Sol) – the seed starts sprouting and growing a stalk and leaves
6. Reaction (Si) – other nearby plants are not so pleased about the space the new sprout is taking up. Change in a situation is not initially welcomed.

7. Establishment (La) – the sprout manages to overcome all obstacles to survival and becomes a well-established tree with many strong roots.

Of course, we need to be prepared for disappointment. Not all seeds sprout and not all sprouts grow to become healthy, well-rooted plants. The eighth step is, in essence, the start of a new phase of evolution, almost like the next level of an upward spiral, so it corresponds to 'favourable circumstances'. This law has much more depth to it than presented here and is worth dedicating some time to explore it further. This law was one of Russian philosopher P.D. Ouspensky's main teachings.

The above pathway is by no means a conclusive collection of the universal truths. For instance, you may also wish to investigate the 'Law of Three', which is mentioned in the Ancient Indian epic 'Mahābhārata' and refers to the existence of three forces when we engage in any endeavor: passive, active and neutral. All three form a three plaited rope, and so they are interconnected.

Before moving on, I would advise you to take some time to contemplate and explore how these laws and universal truths apply to you. What manifestations of these can you see in your own life? Are you in sync with or moving against these truths?

The Garden of Your Mind

Imagine you are meeting your partner's parents for the first time. As you both enter their house, you focus your awareness on how tidy and clean everything is. Not a speck of dust anywhere to be seen. The mother greets you with a handshake and asks you to put on a pair of slippers. The father hugs you and shows you into the living room. Now, depending on the way you represent the world internally (*internal representation system*, or IRS), and how your body chemicals react to your IRS, the meeting with the parents will leave you in a positive or negative emotional state.

Our IRS determines how we perceive reality. Dr. Mihaly Csikszentmihalyi, famous for his book *Flow*, proved that more than two million pieces of information come 'towards' us every second (sounds, images, smells, tactile sensory information, etc.), and so, in order to remain sane, we use filters to choose what information is necessary for us to function. From the two million pieces, our senses can only 'cope' with about seven bits of information per second. This means that the whole of what could be *reality* is reduced, by our specific choice, to seven bits of information into *our reality*. We each choose these bits of information by:

1. **Deleting:** We omit certain aspects of our experience. So, in the 'meeting of the parents' example, the main information retained upon entry in their home was related to the visual representation of the interior of a house. No sounds, no smells and no tactile information was absorbed by the IRS filters.
2. **Distorting:** We filter the information in a distorted way, so we believe we see something that is not there. I'm currently working on my phobia of snakes. In the past, however, when I saw a curved dark line stretched on the road, I would immediately perceive this to be a snake, even though it was in reality a rubber watering pipe.
3. **Generalising:** Once we learn how one person behaves, we assume that this person will continue to behave in the same way, or that every other person who reminds us in some way of that person will behave in the same way. Likewise, once we learn how something functions, we assume that everything

that falls into the same category of this particular object also functions in the same way. Therefore, everything that enters through our eyes, for example, must fit into a category in our brain's library.

Now, there are four filters we use for deleting, distorting and generalising. These filters determine how we personally *decide and choose* our seven bits of information per second:

1. **Values:** They determine the way we make evaluations and set priorities in our daily life. We will see below that they are an essential part of who we are, and they inform our beliefs. If, for instance, one of my top life values is 'remaining in close connection with nature' then I might choose to spend more time with people who share the same *top value* as myself and, during a busy day, to always find time to be with nature.

2. **Beliefs:** These often *unconscious* generalisations of our world form *our* reality. Although beliefs will be discussed in more detail in the section that follows, an example of a belief would be that 'People are generally lazy and only work for money.' How do you think this belief would affect one's life and reality in a workplace context?

3. **Memories**: We usually react to situations based on the memory of our past experiences. For instance, a young woman finds herself at a market shopping for groceries and needs to calculate what change to expect from her transaction. She freezes and is unable to do so, as she recalls memories of her very strict maths teacher in school, and how useless and fearful of making mistakes she felt at the time when it came to doing calculations. Another example of the effect of memories on our behavior would be the same woman walking down the street and spotting from a distance another woman

that she hasn't seen for a number of years. She hurriedly walks towards her to greet her with a huge smile because she holds fond memories from a summer camp they attended together when they were twelve.

4. **Meta-programs**: There are ways by which we manage processes. So, for instance, our meta-program might be that we prefer to avoid pain (we pull away from pain) or that we seek pleasure (we go towards pleasure).

EXERCISE #4
Self-exploration – How memories shape our current behavior

Could you think of similar examples of how your behavior in the present has often been determined by your past memories?

Make a note of at least six such examples (five positive and one negative memory).

Basing yourself on this knowledge, I would like you to now imagine you are a highly esteemed female landscape gardener, like Sabine de Barra in the movie *A little Chaos* (2014), and that before starting a design you have a vision of what you would like this garden to look like: beautiful roses on the periphery, orchard trees, blossoming azaleas and jasmine in the centre, cascading wisterias, and so on. The land you have given is, however, full of boulders, weeds and wild bushes. So, the first thing you would need to do is clear all the unwanted plants and rocks out of the way to give structure and flow to your creation. The plants you want to keep and the ones you want to add would need space, would they not?

You could see your mind in this way. The weeds and rocks represent the values that do not empower you: your limiting beliefs and the ill-perceived memories, or memories of a conflict or event that shocked in the past, causing you a phobia. In contrast, the beautiful roses, jasmine and orchard trees would represent the beliefs that *do* empower you: the values that guide you to become a better self, the memories of receiving and giving pure love and compassion, or lessons from challenging experiences. And so you see that, as the Supreme Gardener of your mind, you have the choice of what stays and what goes. It is your decision, your choice!

> **'As the Supreme Gardener of your mind, you have the choice of what stays and what goes. It is your decision, your choice!'**

The Conscious and the Unconscious Mind

'My life is a story of the self-realisation of the unconscious. Everything in the unconscious seeks outward manifestation, and the personality too desires to evolve out of its unconscious conditions and to experience itself as a whole.' This is how renowned psychiatrist, psychoanalyst and philosopher Carl Jung starts his work, *Memories, Dreams, Reflections* (1995, p.17).

Jung's beautiful reflection suggests that this 'garden' of ours may be much more complex than we imagine. According to cognitive neuroscience, almost 95 percent of how we act, feel, behave and make decisions happens at the non-conscious level of processes, which we are not aware of. This leaves the self-conscious mind responsible for less than 5 percent of our cognitive activity, otherwise known as *executive functions*. In our brain, the self-conscious mind operates in the neocortex area. I wonder which area of our brain our unconscious mind operates in? This may be a trick question ...

'Brave is the one that is not afraid of one's Self.'

Chögyam Trungpa

Have you ever felt frustrated because you feel you really want to achieve a goal and 'something', an unseen force, seems to keep blocking your way?

The conscious mind (often called 'our logic') is the one that sets a goal, such as: 'I will start taking regular breaks throughout my workday', whereas the unconscious mind is the one that will give us the impetus to take these regular breaks. In other words, the unconscious mind will 'get us' the goal. The following illustration demonstrates the power of our unconscious mind as the 'Go-Getter'.

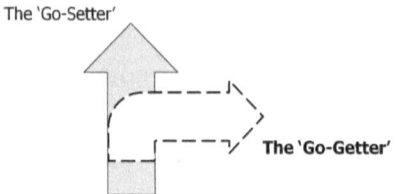

Conscious mind – the 'Go-Setter',
Unconscious Mind – the 'Go-Getter'

Over the years, our mind gets clogged up with 'internal' material which is 'non-recyclable garbage'. This accumulates in the 'cupboard' of our unconscious mind. (Earlier we called it the 'weeds and rocks' of our garden. Here for a better understanding, I will use the 'garbage/cupboard' metaphor.)

In our example of a goal, it is the actual garbage that gets in the way of us not managing to change our habit of working non-stop for long hours. So, we would identify as 'garbage' disempowering beliefs such as: 'If I take a break from what I'm doing, I'm lazy' or 'By taking a break, I interrupt the flow and then I have to start the job from the beginning again.' Often, low self-esteem and feelings of guilt can be a major stumbling block in achieving a goal and, in this example, it would manifest through negative self-talk such as: 'People like me do not deserve breaks', 'Work comes first and my needs come second', or 'I'm a lazy person.' Garbage can also take the form of phobias – for example, the boss catching you out taking a break and thinking you do not deserve the job.

It is vital that we frequently explore our 'unconscious mind-cupboard', especially its darker, deeper corners, so as to clear out the garbage and become free-spirited, compassionate leaders. The more we clear our unconscious mind of phobias, disempowering beliefs and feelings of guilt, the more clarity we have in our thoughts, the more positive are our emotions, the healthier our bodies, and the closer we will get to our wise, authentic, true self.

So, before moving on, let us shine a torch in this 'cupboard', which besides garbage also contains many treasures. In our unconscious minds are:

- All our memories, which are organised and stored. All painful memories, especially childhood memories, are hidden even deeper than others, yet the unconscious mind is ready to recall them when we can face them and transmute them into life lessons.
- All our emotions and the memories of our emotions.
- Our body's blueprint for perfect health. Access to this means we can self-heal.
- Our code of ethics. This is where our value system resides.
- Our beliefs: the limiting and the empowering beliefs about life, people, the world around us, etc.

The unconscious mind is the transmitter and receiver of our perceptual reality. It is better accessed when we are in deep relaxation. This is where our very useful, sixth sense abilities lie (premonition, telepathy, intuition, etc.). It also is the producer of our habitual patterns. No wonder some have gone as far as naming the unconscious mind 'The Boss'. The exercise below offers a revealing demonstration of its powers over our conscious mind, our emotions and our bodily sensations:

EXERCISE #5

Self-Influence towards authenticity –
A slice of lemon and our mind

Choose a restful and calm moment during your day and sit on a chair. Relax, keeping your back straight, with your hands gently resting on your thighs. You can close your eyes if you want.

Imagine there is a table in front of you, and on it is a lemon already sliced in the middle, still cold from the refrigerator. Then, imagine picking up one of the two slices of lemon. You may be able to imagine feeling its cold and wet texture on your fingers.

After you smell it, imagine you are biting into it. What is the feeling in your mouth when you make create thought? Did you feel anything else in your body?

How many other times do we all create thoughts which are so intense that our body thinks our little scenario is actually really happening to us?

Next time you find it hard to 'pass through narrow doors', question whether this is your often phobic conscious mind speaking or

whether they really ARE narrow!

Values

Borrowing from the 'Mean End Chain Theory' of consumer behavior, I would now like to illustrate how deep inside of us are our *values,* and how significant they are in determining our beliefs, the way we do things (strategies), our perception and development of our capabilities, and, finally, what the world sees of us or our behaviors.

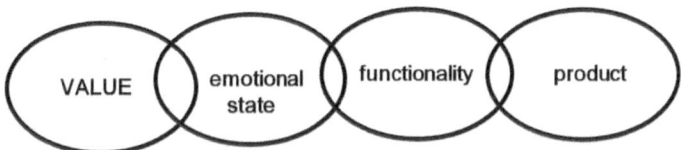

'Means to an End Theory' for Consumer Values

If, for instance, I value a healthy eating lifestyle, then eating healthy food generates a happy emotional state in me, so I buy food that has healthy nutrients and is fresh, locally grown and in season. (One of the products I personally choose to buy, which matches my value of a 'healthy eating lifestyle', is locally grown, organic lettuce.) *Everything* we do or say is a means to an end for us to fulfill one of our values; this is how important they are in our life.

Values start forming during childhood and continue to form, evolve or change completely after major, impactful or challenging events during our lifetime. It is worth noting that some values may no longer serve us and start to disempower us if we do not update them. Also, when the motivation for serving a value is an 'away motion', then this value drains our energy. For instance, if we seek a partner in order to avoid being on our own, then the value of 'companionship' is not helpful in creating a healthy relationship with that partner, as we are constantly in a 'needy' state of receiving instead of in a balanced state of giving/receiving. Contrary to this, a value of 'service', which is motivated to see the pain of others lifted, has a 'towards motion', so it has an empowering, uplifting effect on us.

We often think we already know what our life values are. When asked, we may say: 'Telling the truth' or 'My family', but this is only a vague appreciation of how these values could become a compass for the time we spend on certain activities on a daily basis, and how we can live in sync with them. Also, we may think that the people we work with, or our friends, have the same or similar values as us, especially if we get along well with them. This is not always the case. As mentioned before, another myth about values is that they remain the same throughout our lifetimes. Values change depending on how our beliefs about happiness and success change at different stages of our life, and, particularly, after life-changing events.

The iceberg image that follows may give you an appreciation of the crucial role values play is shaping our existence, influencing our beliefs, thoughts, actions and interactions in the world. Values often act as powerful motivators. They determine how we make choices on a daily basis and generate the strategies we follow to take decisions, even the most mundane ones. Our strategies combined with our capabilities influence our behaviours. Behaviours are the visible part of ourselves to the outside world. They are what people see and this is why in this illustration they are 'above sea level'.

Now, notice how deep beneath the water's surface values are. They are not obvious to others and sometimes, as mentioned previously, not obvious even to ourselves. To be consciously aware of them we need to undergo some serious introspection. In the iceberg illustration, values are purposefully positioned very closely to our 'identity'. This is because our values reflect what we consider important and help define who we are. They guide us to answering the most fundamental question: 'Who am I?' and are therefore intrinsically linked to our life's purpose. Therefore, by reflecting what we consider important our values help define who we are.

When our behaviours, words and actions align with our values, we experience a sense of purpose and fulfilment. Living in accordance with our values, is in essence 'Living Our Truth' and this is what gives our lives meaning and direction.

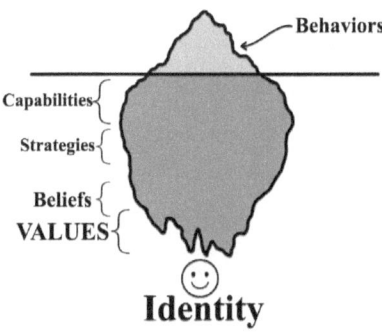

The Values Iceberg

The following six-stage exercise will help you identify or confirm your three most significant values. Focusing on the top three gives you more clarity and a compass for knowing how to navigate through a stressful day and still remain on course to live a more fulfilling, compassionate life, where 'giving to others' is effortless and a pleasure. Knowing your current values contributes towards living a life without contradictions, guilt and fear.

This exercise requires a fair amount of time to do (2–3 hours). It is, however, one of the most powerful self-exploration exercises you will ever do.

EXERCISE #6

Self-exploration –
Eliciting your top three life values

Practicalities: For stage D especially (see below), it is best that you record your values for each of the stages A to C in a Word document, so that you can easily copy and paste them when it is time for stage E ('Identifying the top three values'). Alternatively, if you do not have access to a computer, it is possible to do stage E manually, but make sure that you leave a gap under each experience that you write down. It is also highly recommended that you choose to do this exercise when you are relaxed and alone.

STAGE A: Experiences relating to paid work

By reflecting on the past two to three years, identify times when you were employed or self-employed and were doing or experiencing something on your own or with business partners, suppliers or colleagues. Make a note of two such events, one each for: a time when you were most proud of yourself, a time when one of your deepest need or desire was fulfilled, and a time when you felt joyous. Try to describe these events in as much detail as possible by noting the emotions you felt, the people you were with, the places these happened, what skills you used (e.g., hands, mental, social). If going back two to three years does not yield any such memories, then you can go back five to ten years.

STAGE B: Experiences relating to family, friends, social/voluntary activities

Go back over the past two or three years to times when you were with your friends or family or doing volunteer work or communal activities. Identify and make a note of two such experiences, one each for: a time when you were most proud of yourself, a time when one of your deepest needs or desires was fulfilled, and a time when you felt fortunate and happy. Make sure you describe these experiences in as much detail as possible by noting the emotions you felt, the people you were with, where this took place, the atmosphere, the weather, etc.

If going back two to three years does not produce any such experiences, then you can go back five to ten years. If this is the case, this could be an indication and a useful self-knowledge hint relating to an imbalance in the time you spend with family or communicating and socialising with other people in general.

STAGE C: Experiences of a personal nature

Think back over the past two or three years of times when you were alone, or doing or experiencing something on your own or with strangers (i.e., not with friends, family or colleagues). Identify and make a note of two such events, one each for: a time when you were most proud of yourself, a time when one of your deepest needs or desires was fulfilled, and a time when you felt blissful and radiant. Describe each memory in as much detail as possible by noting what you felt, how it all started, the places you were at and its ambience, what skills, if any, you used.

If going back two to three years does not initiate any such memories, then you can go back five to ten years. If this is the case, this could be an indication and a useful self-knowledge hint relating to an imbalance in the time you spend with yourself on your own.

STAGE D: Identifying the values relating to each of the above experiences

At this stage you need to read back through all your experiences, then look at the list of values below and write down on a separate sheet of paper or in a Word document at least four values that you think relate to each experience, and what made it stand out from the rest. If you come up with a value that is not on the list, feel free to use it.

Additional tips: If some values seem similar to you, choose the word that describes it more accurately. Try to be consistent. For example, 'inner-harmony' and 'balance' almost mean the same thing. If two or more experiences relate to these values, always choose one of the two and the same one each time (i.e., choose 'balance' for all relevant experiences). Also, for values that are made up of two or three words, use a dash between the words, such as for 'personal-responsibility'.

STAGE E: Identifying the top three key values

A/ If you are doing the self-assessment manually, without the use of a Word document to record the values from the previous stages, proceed with the following:

accountability	Excitement	perfection
accuracy	expertise	personal-responsibility
achievement	exploration	positivity
adventure	expressiveness	practicality
altruism	fairness	preparedness
ambition	faith	prestige
assertiveness	family	productivity
autonomy	fidelity	professionalism
audacity	fitness	prudence
agility	fluency	quality
balance	focus	relationship
beauty	freedom	reliability
being-the-best	fun	resourcefulness
belonging	generosity	respect
boldness	goodness	restraint
calmness	grace	results-oriented
carefulness	greatness	reverence
candour	gratitude	rigor
challenge	growth	security
cheerfulness	happiness	self-actualisation
clear-mindedness	hard-work	self-control
commitment	health	selflessness
communication	helping-others	self-reliance
community	holiness	sensitivity
compassion	honesty	serenity
competition	honour	service
consistency	humility	shrewdness
connection	humour	simplicity
contentment	independence	soundness
continuous-improvement	ingenuity	speed
contribution	inner-harmony	spirituality
control	innovation	spontaneity
cooperation	inquisitiveness	stability
correctness	insightfulness	strategic
courage	integrity	strength
courtesy	intelligence	structure
creativity	intellectual-status	success
curiosity		support
decisiveness	intuition	temperance
dependability	joy	thankfulness
determination	justice	thoroughness

devoutness	knowledge	thoughtfulness
diligence	leadership	timeliness
discipline	legacy	tolerance
discretion	leisure	traditionalism
diversity	love	tranquillity
duty	loyalty	trustworthiness
dynamism	nature	truth-seeking
economy	making-a-difference	understanding
efficiency		uniqueness
elegance	mastery	unity
empathy	merit	usefulness
enjoyment	obedience	variety
enthusiasm	openness	vision
entrepreneurship	order	vitality
equality	originality	wealth
excellence	passion	wisdom
	partnership	
	patriotism	

1. Look through the list of all the values you noted on the separate sheet of paper, irrespective of which category of experiences they came from.
2. First, circle the ones, if any, that occur more than once. Use different colour pens for each value type.
3. Then see which single value from each experience you would choose as being the strongest and most representative of the four or five words that you originally noted. Highlight this.
4. See if you observe any patterns. Are there four or five words/values that keep repeating?
5. If yes, copy them down separately on another blank

sheet of paper and see if you can minimise them down to three values. If not, check whether you have used synonyms to describe the same meaning of certain values. Replace the synonyms by choosing the one word that is closest and review your list again for occurrences of the same word. If necessary, repeat actions 2–4.
6. If you have less than ten words, try to choose the top three values by prioritising them.

B/ If you are doing the self-assessment with the use of a computer and are using a Word document to record the values from the previous stages, proceed with the following:

1. Copy and paste the list of all the values you wrote in your Word document, irrespective of which category of experiences they came from, into the free online wordle tool found at this link http://www.wordle.net/create Beforehand, make sure that only spaces separate each word/value from one another and that values made from two words are joined with a dash. Also, if you are having problems creating the 'word cloud' of text, make sure your browser is using the latest version of Java.
2. This beautiful image should clearly show your top three values. If two values are in the same priority, then keep both of them and allow yourself to have four key values If, after using wordle, you are still not clear about your top three values, then print out the

whole list of values and follow the steps described above for manually identifying the top three.

STAGE F: Reality check – Are you living by your values?

This is the most valuable part of the exercise and a great contribution towards reinforcing your self-leadership skills. Here, you need to allocate some time for introspection in order to assess whether your daily activities, the job you do, the friends you have, and the way you spend your free time are in sync with your key values.

When you live by your values, you:

1. are confident you are making the right decisions
2. feel there is integrity in your words and actions
3. are not stressed by what people think of what you say and do
4. become more outspoken and do not shy away from sharing these values with people, so they know your limits
5. you can consciously say 'no' to activities that do not support your values, so you manage your time better. You know how to identify the significant activities during your day
6. you can consciously 'clear' your life of people that oppose your values, or at least minimise contact with them.

> You will discover many more benefits after completing this exercise. One last note, since values may change during our lifetime, it is wise to repeat this process every two to five years or after a life-changing event.

Another equally effective way to elicit values is to ask the question of every area of your life: 'What is important?' So, for instance: 'What is important about your career?'

Beliefs

On a personal level, the formation of beliefs takes place right throughout our lifetimes. Psychologists claim, however, that the majority of these are subconsciously formed up to the age of seven when, just as sponges do, we absorb everything we sense, hear or see, and we model our world based on how our parents or other people in our close environment behave. From a much wider, systemic angle, we also develop beliefs which are related to our genealogy (our ancestors), society, religion, country, race, sex, or even related to our whole species.

As shocking as it may seem to you, a *belief* that some of us have absorbed and has proven to be limiting is that, as we age, the cells in our body die and the functions of our organs (including our brain) diminishes. There are now many examples throughout history of people who have reached beyond 120 years of age and passed away only because they *decide* to do so. At this point, I would like to remind you, as explained earlier, that *we decide and choose* how we delete, distort and generalise the information that comes in through our sensory awareness. If only we could *choose* to 'see' our world through the eyes of our heart!

Another example of how beliefs work would be when a teacher has the belief that a child is 'good', then the child will most likely interact with the teacher as a well-behaved child would.

An alternative and more dynamic way of viewing our beliefs, especially in relation to manifestation, is to identify the beliefs we would need to adopt in order to make our dreams come true. This is positive psychology. And the opposite strategy would be to identify the beliefs that we think are obstacles to what we want to manifest. The danger here may be that we go looking for beliefs that are not really ours, telling ourselves that if our dream hasn't yet materialised then we are bound to be blocking it from happening ourselves with our negative thinking. This may not be true, as there are many reasons why our wishes have not happened yet. For example, maybe the players of our dream scene are not yet 'in position' or ready for us, or maybe the universe has something a lot better 'slow-cooking' in the background. So, a positive psychology exercise to put you in the right mindset is offered below. This will prepare you for your visualisation practices, , such as the ones suggested at the end of this chapter.

> **EXERCISE #7**
>
> **Self-influence towards authenticity – What beliefs would you have if you were a billionaire?**
>
> Find a quiet corner and jot down on a piece of paper or your notebook what it is you would like to manifest. It can be something small or your BIG life dream, a business, a partner, a journey, etc. Make sure you express it in the present tense, as if it has already happened.
>
> Next, and without overthinking, write beneath your dream five beliefs that you would be holding if your dream was now a reality. For example, what thoughts would you have about money if you were a billionaire? For example, 'Money is currency and needs to flow in and flow out', 'Money is abundant, so there is enough wealth for all people to have access to it', 'The more money I have, the more people I can help by putting it to good use.'
>
> You could use these sentences as positive affirmations and get them, for example, onto a poster in Canva.com or transform them into a screensaver. In this way you will have a daily reminder of the mindset that you need to have to reflect your dream life.

The way reality is translated and perceived is not only different amongst humans. In the world of animals, frogs only eat small moving entities. Their visual-neurological system allows them to see the world in limited hues of color, and they hone in on flies in the air. So, a motionless fly sitting right in front of a frog would not enter into its visual perception and would escape being eaten. Moreover, unlike humans, cats and dogs have a physiology that allows them to also hear ultrasounds.

> **'One of the greatest paradoxes of your physical senses is that your eyes actually show you what YOU BELIEVE, not what you see.'**
>
> Mike Dooley

One of the most scientifically sound books I have come across on how our mind connects to our body and the power of beliefs is Dr Deepak Chopra's *Quantum Healing*. And my first choice of a book that shatters our perception of reality, also written by an acclaimed scientist, is Dr. Jeremy Hayward's *Letters to Vanessa*. Both books are written for people with no scientific background and demonstrate that our daily life is a phenomenal world created by our five senses, and that it is simply an illusion (*Maya* in Sanskrit), an individual movie we each project externally, that we each subjectively 'see' as real. From the ancient Vedic *rishis* to Plato in Ancient Greece to quantum physics in modern times, '*consciousness* is the source of reality'.

In the context of leadership, it is worthwhile remembering that the more people imagine the same future reality, the higher the probability of this manifesting in a physical sense. As we will see, this is the power of imagination and vision.

EXERCISE #8

Self-exploration - How friendly is the world to you?

Take a quiet moment and try to answer these simple yes/no questions spontaneously, as honestly as you can and in the present tense. Avoid ambivalent answers such as 'maybe', 'sometimes', 'I am now, but this morning I wasn't ...'

1. Are you totally responsible for your happiness?
2. Do you find Earth to be a friendly place?
3. Do you believe there is no good and evil? That all people are basically good?
4. Do you feel free and in no way trapped by your surroundings, sex, body, health, relationships, family or financial status, job circumstances or any other of your life's aspects?
5. Do you feel respected and listened to?
6. Do you feel creative and free to create?
7. Do you feel you have a significant contribution to make towards the well-being of those around you?
8. Do you feel you show your authentic self and never feel you need to hide who you truly are?
9. Do you feel free from regrets or guilt about an action, a thought, or something you said in the past?
10. Do you believe you are your self's best guide?

The way you answer these will help you identify what beliefs you have that may stand between you and your authentic expression and freedom.

Let me share with you a little story about my own about one of my past disempowering beliefs. The process of releasing it and clearing it took place while I was being trained to be a Neurolinguistic Programming (NLP) Master Practitioner. Here is some background to what happened during that NLP session. I come from a well-educated, middle-class family. My mother is from Wales in the UK and my father is from the island of Crete in Greece. I have a younger brother and sister. I was brought up in Athens and although, as is common with most families, there was a lot of dysfunction in the way we related to each other, we were showered with love.

During the NLP session, my instructor Terry Elston (NLP World Ltd) asked me the following question about a statement I had made about my family: 'When did you decide that men view women as belonging in the kitchen washing dishes and not in work?' Without skipping a beat, I responded that that this was when I was thirteen years old and my father would still not allow my well-educated mother to work. Straight after my response, I had a 'thunder-bolt' moment. I was in charge of making this decision! I was personally responsible for the way I saw reality, and I was responsible for how men reacted to my words and actions, or reactions, in my workplace.

'What we do not know controls us.'

James Hollis in *Under Saturn's Shadow*

All these years, my complaint in work had always been that my colleagues in my all-male department ignored me when I spoke –

they simply did not listen! My father did not listen, my ex-husband did not listen, my partners did not listen. What an unfriendly place this world was for me! And there were men everywhere! Yet, I could not imagine a world without them. So, I was seriously stuck! I had a mouth to speak but apparently, in my mind, my voice was less than a whisper.

Now it is time we try you out on some of your subjective views of the world. This exercise needs to be done in a fun and spontaneous way.

EXERCISE # 9

Self-exploration – What do you believe?

Complete these sentences without thinking about them too much, but answer in an honest and spontaneous way. Do not spend more than ten minutes on this exercise.

1. My life is ...
2. I am ...
3. My body is ...
4. I see money as ...
5. Love is ...
6. Men are ...
7. Friendship is ...
8. People are ...
9. Success is ...
10. I am happy when ...

> The way you answer these will reflect the perception you have of the world in the present moment. Contemplate which of these responses make you feel expanded and free, and which make you feel contracted and trapped within conditions that you have no control over (e.g., 'I am happy when the people around me are happy').
>
> The last category stems from limiting beliefs. So, what you could do next to re-condition your brain, is to try and re-write the sentences that cultivate limiting beliefs, so that they free you from negative perceptions.
>
> This exercise is worth revisiting in about a month's time to notice if something has changed in the way you see the world.

Phobias and Fear

Two years ago, I was at the funeral of my beloved uncle, and I felt the fear of death all around me. This is a primitive fear, common for most of us and not very easy to control. In this section, I would like to discuss some other strong emotions that can have a paralysing effect over us, and that we also tend to call 'fears', even though, in reality, they are 'phobias'. Examples of phobias would be: darkness, heights, insects, being out of our depth in the sea (drowning), physical pain, losing one's senses, public speaking, etc.

Real fear is what we feel, for example, when we see an oncoming vehicle. Fortunately for us, there is such a feeling as fear because this is what gives the signal to the amygdala part of our brain to 'take flight' and get out of the vehicle's way. In contrast, obsessing over our phobia can drive us crazy and eventually even kill us, for when we let it dominate us mentally, we now know that it can poison our body with toxins, causing serious illnesses or leading us to make knee-jerk reactions, such as running away from an imaginary thief, only to end up crossing the street and get knocked over by a passing car.

The difference between real fear and a phobia is that we create phobias in our mind by distorting, deleting or generalising the information in the world around us. We do this because, as we have already discussed, each person decides to internalise different pieces of information about reality – phobias are highly subjective. In other words, what may be a phobia to one may sound ridiculous to another. Phobias are also highly contagious, as with any strong emotion. Eliminating your phobias can be very empowering and freeing, especially if, as a woman, you are afraid of voicing your opinion in a meeting where decisions are made, doing a presentation in front of prospective clients, or teaching your child to become independent of you.

To help you work with your phobias, here are two exercises with this purpose in mind.

EXERCISE #10

Self-influence towards authenticity
– The 'two chair' workout of phobias

For this exercise, you need to be alone and will need two empty chairs. It can take from between fifteen and thirty minutes. Choose one of your *less debilitating* phobias and see if you can play this game.

> First, place the chairs facing each other, then sit on one of the chairs and talk to the other as if someone else is sitting opposite you. Express what it is that you are afraid of and where you feel the fear in your body. Then change chairs and become a five-year-old girl who talks about her phobia to the now grown-up, adult 'you'. Change positions once more and see what you would say to the little 'you' as an adult in order to reassure her.
>
> Notice what you will discover!

As a first-aid solution, when you are scared and panicking, use your imagination and put yourself in a ball of light. This image will calm you down and protect you. You can do the same for all your loved ones that you feel are at risk or even for people that are attacking you. The ball of light knows no distances and no time! Play a little!

More of the stronger negative emotions, such as anger and anxiety, will be discussed in the following chapters.

> **EXERCISE # 11**
>
> Self-influence towards authenticity
> – Shattering your phobias
>
> For this exercise, you will need to find a quiet space with a table and chair, two sheets of blank A4 paper, a pencil

and rubber, a and ruler or book to help you make straight lines. Doing this exercise manually instead of electronically will provide you with a more experiential and meaningful experience. I would also recommend that you read the whole list of instructions so that you know where you are heading, so to speak.

Once you are in your chosen space and ready to start, attach or glue the two A4 sheets, to provide you with a larger 'canvas' to write on. Next, use some method to concentrate and become present; for example, meditation or breathwork. This does not have to be for long, a maximum of three to four minutes. In this present state, ask yourself what your two most important phobias in your life right now. On your blank sheet, draw a spacious table with nine columns and two rows, one row for each phobia. Now, place the following titles in each column:

1. Short phobia description: Describe precisely what it is that you are afraid of, and if you can, note how intense this phobia is from 1 to 100, (e.g., 'fear of darkness when alone': 70/100).
2. Bodily symptoms: When you feel afraid due to this phobia, what symptoms does it cause in your body? Set tension rates for the discomfort you normally feel (e.g., 'stomach pain, blood pressure rockets up': 90/100 intensity).
3. Whose model is this phobia from? Phobias are often linked to childhood memories of a shocking event that is trapped in our unconscious, or it can also be that one of our parents has the same phobia

and we have 'modeled' it off them. Ask yourself whether one of your parents has this phobia. Make a note of this discovery. To untrap and release a shocking past memory, you may need the help of an experienced professional (e.g., an NLP Master Practitioner).

4. Scenarios: When you think of what you are phobic of, what are the different stories ('movies', scenarios) that you play out in your mind? Which of them is the worst? Make a note of it in detail.

5. Realistic odds: How likely is it that your worst-case scenario will happen? Analyse whether each of the elements that make up this scenario is based on real statistical probabilities. For instance, if you are phobic that you will have a heart attack because a close relative had one and died, ask yourself: 'How many people who feel pain in their chest died from a heart attack, based on medical scientific evidence?' If you have noted another scenario that you would like to explore factually, then do so and note a percentage of the realistic probability of each scenario occurring in your own lifetime.

6. Precautions: What precautions could you take to prevent each scenario from happening? Which people around you could you ask for help? What self-talk could you engage in regularly in order to take control of your emotions and calm yourself down?

7. Feeling: If one of the scenarios really does happen, what do you think you will feel, and in which area

> of your body will this feeling mirror itself in? Make a note of the intensity it might have.
> 8. 'First Aid': If one of the scenarios actually occurs, what options would you have available at the time?
> 9. Intensity after exercise: How do you feel NOW about this old phobia? What is its intensity on a scale of 1 to 100? How does this score compare with the one in step 1 above?
>
> If you found this helpful, you can repeat the same process for your second phobia.

Thoughts

When we spot a close relative from a distance, we cannot simply explain this biologically just by saying that we simply 'saw' them using our eyes. In fact, according to quantum biology and neuroscience, millions of electrical messages go through our brain, igniting a chemical reaction that, with the help of neurotransmitters, light up many of our other organs besides the brain. From a physiological standpoint, the cortex part of our brain is where the thinking takes place (executive function), including language, logic, interpretation, sense perception and sense interconnection. It is divided into the left and right hemispheres, and they control movement and sensations in the opposite sides of our body.

Each hemisphere also controls different thinking functions. The left is used more for analytical, quantity-related thinking and goal setting (planning of steps, direction, mapping and more masculine energy 'thinking styles'), whereas the right is used more for holistic, quality-related thinking (creativity, imagination, intuition, foresight, pattern and trend detection abilities). As mentioned already, this is an oversimplified and segregated description of our thinking function, and it is necessary to steer away from assuming that the brain equates to a mind. Thanks to the work of scientists such as Dr Deepak Chopra, Dr Bruce Lipton and Dr Donald D. Hoffman (University of California), we now know that every single cell of our body has a mind of its own, so thoughts are not restricted to the area of the human brain, not even in the confines of matter. Irrespective of how hard we try to capture the genius of Mozart's composing streak, we will not be able to emulate it by searching its source in the body.

Have you ever heard these expressions? 'My mind is all over the place', 'Park that thought', 'On second thoughts', 'Think positive'. Thoughts are constant and, in my experience, it is almost impossible while awake to stop their flow, even when sitting on the meditation cushion. Thoughts are either 'of the past' or 'of the future'. They have no home in the NOW, even though such a state of presence would be a highly desirable and healthy state to be in, as it is the best way to connect us to our true self, to be heart-led and to radiate compassion.

So, how do we become friends with our 'thinking' function and use it for what it is meant to be used for, such as sending positive thoughts to people around us, producing encouraging thoughts to motivate ourselves, for planning a project, or for finding a solution to a challenge? And when do we get a chance to rest during our busy day, a chance to create that blissful silence, that space that allows us to feel free, safe and loved? When do we 'indulge' in *maitri* (Sanskrit word meaning loving-kindness)?

Below are some ways that I have found effective and that you may wish to explore and try out for yourself.

Mindfulness meditation would be my first choice of practice to become friends with my thoughts and their accompanying emotions. Mindfulness meditation cultivates self-compassion. It encourages curiosity about ourselves in a non-judgmental way. Some days my thoughts flow like Niagara Falls and I make whole 'life movies' with them, while on other days they trickle like a leaky tap and I just watch them 'come in' and 'fly out' again. I finally decided that the more I try to suppress them or send them away, the more persistent they become. One of my mindfulness instructors used to say: 'You can allow your thoughts to come, but you do not have to invite them in for tea!'

'You cannot control the mind, whereas you can choose to 'let go' of your thoughts!'

With mindfulness meditation, you keep your eyes open, aware of your world and your attention is more on the out-breath. Providing you are sitting upright and adopt the correct posture, you are in a better position when thoughts and emotions come to simply notice yourself thinking, and then sim-ply label the thought 'thinking', and then gently bring your attention back to the breath. The idea is to 'touch and go' or to simply 'let go' of your thoughts, not blocking them from entering. The purpose of mentioning such a practice here is by no means to train you on how to do it simply by reading these instructions. It is necessary to experience it for yourself and it is best to do so under the guidance of a meditation instructor. Nevertheless, mindfulness meditation has been one of the most influential tools for me to remain in the present moment, in the NOW. It then becomes more of a *state of being* rather than a tool or a daily practice.

Moreover, every time we consciously stop our activity and make a conscious effort to focus on our breath, we not only benefit ourselves but also benefit all sentient beings in our surroundings and make a contribution towards raising the vibration of our planet.

PRACTICE #3
Self-exploration and Self-influence – Haiku poetry

If you want to explore another side of yourself and also train the mind to focus and be creative, then I highly recommend you try out Haiku poetry, a Japanese verse in three lines. Line one has five syllables, line two has seven syllables and line three has five syllables. If, like myself, you are not very good at counting syllables, you can use an online counter.

I will share with you one of my poems (almost ... a haiku!), called 'Flickering':

> **Harrowing circles trap**
> **fickle butterflies in stormy nets**
> **candles blown in summer's winds.**

The *NOW state*® is a way of *being*, maybe the only true way of existing and connecting to reality as it is in the present. I experienced it under the guidance of my NLP instructor, Terry Elston.

I would not call it a 'practice' as it is a state of being, although it does require constant effort and practice. The concept of the *NOW state* is used by many high-achieving athletes, as it increases concentration and heightens all your senses, including our sixth sense (intuition, premonition, etc.). The result of being in the NOW is the same as the split second of a gap between the out-breath and the in-breath during mindfulness meditation, or any conscious, deep breathing for that matter, or the merging of our being whilst experiencing a beautiful sunset. In this state, you allow for the whiteness of space to exist. You can embrace the unknown, fear, pain, any emotion, and you can also relate and serve others in a truly helpful, compassionate way.

Silence and *connection with Mother Nature*. I have always found this to be a great combination therapy for calming a busy, worried mind. One of my most life-changing lessons was going on a 'Vision Quest' in North Wales, UK (www.ancienthealingways.co.uk). There, under the guidance of our teacher Pippa Bondy, each 'seeker' had to survive on their own for five days in a tent on the slopes of Snowdonia, with only water, a pen and a notebook for journaling. At about the third day, there was an amazing shift in my consciousness. All of my senses were heightened, as if I had become the 'Bionic Woman'! My normal thinking pattern was seriously but pleasantly 'disrupted' by the silence inside of me. Nature did its best to keep her volume up: howling winds, torrential rain, buzzing bees. Nevertheless, I somehow felt embraced and protected by her, and there, in the silence of my heart, I forgave myself, forgave others, got fearful, laughed, explored my limitations and saw my beauty.

'Listen to the Wind ... It carries all the answers.'

'Vision Quest' is a rite of passage ceremony that resembles what used to take place naturally amongst ancient tribes all over the world. By exploring our relationship with nature, we explore our relationship with both our light and darkness. This profound experience helps us to appreciate the point in life we are at, and how we transit from one stage to another. Without allowing time for such experiences, we go through life in a flash and miss out on tasting life's beautiful flavour and seeing our own magnificence.

If you do not feel ready for such an experience, I would highly recommend that you go into nature for a few hours per week – and why not? Lay all your worries on the trees or send them gushing away in the river. Make sure, however, that you listen to the wind. It carries all the answers ...

According to UK's forest bathing scientific expert, Dr Kirsten McEwan, and researchers from Japan (which is the country of origin of *Shinrin-yoku*, as it is called in Japanese), the continued practice of regularly engaging the senses in a forest or woods for at least twenty minutes can increase overall well-being and result in increased heart rate variability, positive emotions and levels of compassion towards others, and it can reduce moodiness and rumination. With her work, Kirsten and her team even managed to get forest bathing socially prescribed by Guildford Council in the UK, aiming for it to become part of the British government's green social prescribing programme. Another team of scientists proved that a day trip to a forest park increases the cells that act as natural killers of bad cells within our body (natural killer cells, also known as NK cells) and reinforces the expression of anti-cancer proteins.

Journaling has now become a permanent daily practice since the 'Vision Quest' experience. I find that making a note of my thoughts and emotions first thing in the morning, in this semi-relaxed state, surpasses the otherwise yapping 'monkey mind' and allows me access to my unconscious mind, which then becomes a doorway to my soul. Here are a few reasons why it is a good idea to journal:

1. It allows you to see problems in a new light and open out new, creative possibilities that daytime logic would dismiss or even miss altogether.
2. By noting thoughts and feelings, a poem, or an imaginary story, you start understanding yourself more and your wishes and dislikes. It cultivates intuitive writing.
3. You allow time to be with yourself. You feel special and develop a stronger identity of 'self'. So, journaling is a great confidence and self-esteem booster!
4. It is a way to release emotional burdens and have a shoulder to cry on. It feels as if you are writing to a pen pal, and sometimes the pen pal answers back. Personally, I find that by practising journaling regularly, I now have my own therapist.
5. It helps you become a better communicator. By organising your thoughts on paper, you can then express them to others in a clearer way.
6. It is a record of your life, your timeline and family history. In retrospect, it provides you with a pathway to your own development.

Water crystals and our thoughts. As mentioned earlier, Japanese scientist Dr Emoto Masaru proved, through his extensive research of the formation of water crystals, the effect our thoughts and words have on water. As you may already know, our bodies reflect Earth's water analogies. Our body mass is made up of more than 70 percent water. Positive thoughts, such as 'love and gratitude' (see image on the front cover of Dr Masaru's book) form beautiful, healthy crystals, whereas negative thoughts such as 'I can't do it', 'It is hopeless' and 'I hate you' form dysmorphic, unhealthy crystals. A little practice we can do to improve our health, as suggested by Dr Masaru is to write beautiful, loving words on our water bottles and, better still, to say them out loud so that the vibrations of the words emanate the corresponding emotional energy in all water elements in our vicinity.

Being in the *'Flow'*, studied by the late Dr Mihaly Csikszentmihalyi, is also one of the best ways to remain in a space awareness state, with fewer thoughts whirling about. To get to this state, the secret is finding something you are passionate about and engaging yourself completely in it. I'm sure that most teachers will agree with me on this. Whenever I go into class unprepared, I deliver the best lesson ever, because I'm completely in that 'space', unconfined by limits, connected to the collective wisdom! Cast your mind to a time you had this feeling of 'flow'. We all know what it feels like.

In a practical way, I have found that by directing my attention to my body, to the way it moves and then carefully listening to the messages it sends, I have access to my bodily wisdom. This practice is called 'somatics' and it is one that links us to the sensorial experience of life, increases our grounding and therefore our mindfulness and flow.

On a more holistic level, thoughts have much less power over us when there is 'heart-brain-body coherence'. Many scientists have spoken about the heart's intelligence and how our heart knows what is going to happen before our brain, and, therefore, when the energy pathway that connects the heart to our brain is clear, the heart can inform our brain of the future. Moreover, a bright, young female scientist, Dr Julia Enders, has raised our awareness of the gut's brain and how that affects our emotions, cognitive state and overall well-being. Very conducive to helping raise our awareness and mindfulness is regular bodily exercise. I will be discussing more about the body's contribution to this important need for the 'heart-brain-body coherence' later on.

Befriending our thoughts, not judging ourselves, releasing guilt, self-forgiveness and forgiveness all take considerable effort. Trying to introduce new habits of thinking and ways of being whilst rushing to keep all balls in the air can be overwhelming, so I have found that it is best to choose one new habit change and 'try it on for size' in baby steps. They say that small hinges can make big door swings! Little changes, big shifts!

The 'Tiny Habits' method discovered by Dr Fogg is a good guide to do just this. In his book, he explains how 'tiny' can be transformative. He helps us remember how to neuro-wire the new habit by using an ABC sequence:

'**A**' is for anchoring the habit to an existing routine.
'**B**' is for performing the new behaviour just after the existing routine.
'**C**' is for celebrating the 'good job' you have done immediately after performing the tiny new behaviour.

An example would be: 'After I open my eyes in the morning, I will smile to myself and say, "Today is going to be a great day!"'

On his website, www.TinyHabits.com/1000recipes, you can find a wealth of ideas for a variety of life situations and challenges.

PRACTICE #4
Self-influence towards authenticity
– The four pebbles meditation

'I choose to be as fresh as a flower, steady as a mountain, with a crystal-clear mind of an alpine lake and as free as empty space.' I really like this phrase, which is from the 'Pebble Meditation' performed by monk Thay Phap Luu from Plum Village. It only takes ten minutes to do. You can repeat this practice every time you feel exhausted, fearful, confused or trapped. Thay Phap Luu suggests that we can make this meditation more practical by placing four pebbles in a little pouch and keeping it in our bag, using it or part of it every time we feel unresourceful. I have placed the YouTube link to the meditation performed by Thay Phap Luu at the end of the practice.

Here however I offer a condensed version of the instructions which I would recommend that you use to read out loud once and record them in your own voice. When we listen to our own voice the meditative and calming effect is much more powerful than listening to somebody else's. I have therefore worded them using the first person to make it easier for you to record:

- I find a quiet, comfortable, and safe place. A room where I have removed all electronic devices, or better still, outdoors, in natural surroundings. I sit down calmly, and I focus on the present moment by simply following my natural breath. I open the pouch with

the four pebbles and put it in front of me to the left.
- I pick up the first pebble with my left hand. This pebble represents the flower. At this point it may be easier if I close my eyes. Next, I place the flower pebble in my right hand, closing it in my fist and I say: 'When I breathe in, I am a flower. When I breathe out, I feel fresh, I feel joy.' And indeed, I notice that something is changing inside me. I feel more energy. I then place this first pebble on the ground to my right.
- I pick up a second pebble out of the pouch on my left, using my left hand. This pebble represents the mountain. Following a similar sequence as before, this time I say: When I inhale, I am a mountain. When I exhale, I feel steady. I have strong roots. Nothing can shake me. Whatever emotions come I simply sway right and left, and then return to my solid centre. I repeat this wording as many times as I feel the need to do so.
- I then place the second, mountain pebble on my right on the ground next to the flower pebble and, then with gentle movements, I take the third pebble with my left hand and place it in my right fist.
- As I do this, I imagine it represents the crystal, clear water of an alpine lake as it reflects the sky and I say: "As I breathe in, I am water. As I breathe out, I mirror things just as they are. My mind is calm just like the mountain water and I can see deep inside my mind, its sadness or joy". I take as many breaths as I need until I feel the peace and clarity of crystal mountain water and then leave this third pebble gently by my right side, alongside the other two.

- Finally, I get the fourth, pebble and place it in my right hand. This one represents space. I say: «When I am free, I feel truly happy. I feel space inside me, an expansion. Nothing can stop me. Space allows me to be open just like the blue sky. My mind is open, limitless. I breathe in empty space; I breathe out freedom. I now put the space pebble next to the other three.
- I gently finish off this meditation by sending myself a breeze of Spring's freshness!

I have found this to be a very powerful practice. If you carry the pouch with you during your daily routine, you can if you wish stop once or twice a day and take a few conscious breaths and then place your hand in your pouch and touch one of the four pebbles. By doing so, the physical sensation will act as a trigger and help you transmute the feeling of sadness, confusion, insecurity or anger into joy, freshness, stability and freedom!

(Source: search for 'Pebble Meditation' on YouTube)

Your Reality and the Power of a Vision

By this point, hopefully it has become obvious that our experience and awareness of the world is *subjective* and not merely generated by our brain.

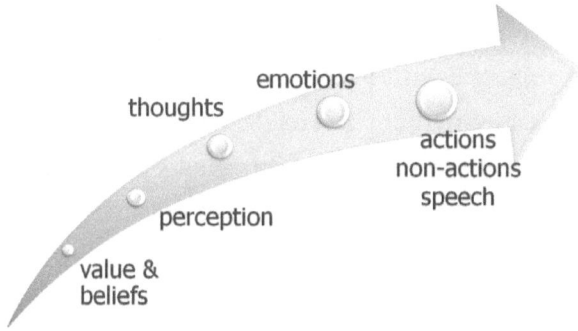

The way you shape your reality

Putting all the pieces together and recalling the iceberg diagram (on page X), we may gradually grasp that it is *us* who shape our reality. This is not only important as far as our own personal experience is concerned, but it is also significant in how we relate to other people. The reaction of two people in the same situation may be different. Remembering that each one of us experiences a different reality would make us less critical of others and reduce our tendency to think that we can mind-read.

Only YOU are responsible for your happiness.

We live at a time when the whole of humanity is at a turning point. As scientist Dr Greg Braden mentions in his talks: 'We are already in the next Age. The Age of Meeting Ourselves Again.' In order to thrive, we need to seek out the values of our ancestors, those who lived many centuries ago. We need to *re-member*. We are all called upon at a personal and collective level to take critical decisions. These critical choices relate to the battle of the 'old way of thinking' with the new one. The 'new way of thinking' – which is in fact very, very old – has its foundations in truth, love and freedom. Any of us who continue to operate with beliefs contrary to these because we feel safe, or we are used to it and feel too lazy to change, will run into difficulties. Our bodies are 'thirsty' for truth, love and freedom. When our body does not quench its thirst, it gets sick. Simple.

On a very positive note, the fact that we create our reality makes us our life's own 'directors'. Our thoughts, words and actions shape our future, opening a whole range of possibilities. Infinite possibilities! All we need to do is let our imagination go wild! Walt Disney, who had a rough start in life, used to say: 'If you can imagine it, then you can make it happen!'.

Taking this a step further, spiritual teacher Wayne Dyer is known to have said that you manifest what you are, not what you wish for. From my own personal experience, ever since having a clear sense of purpose and having a vision of what I want to dedicate my life to, when I think of the 'Sparkles in Young People's Eyes' imagery and the creation of the 'School for Young Leaders', mentioned in the introduction of this book, I feel unstoppable, like a fast-flowing river. In fact, I become that river!

> ## Courage starts with showing up and letting ourselves be seen.
> Brene Brown

The way to find out your purpose is simple, yet it requires a warrior's courage. Experiment, experiment, experiment until you find what your passion is. Open out your possibilities by divergent thinking and seek out new experiences. Get out of your comfort zone. Keep knocking on doors! One of them will open.

EXERCISE #12
Self-influence towards authenticity – Draw your vision

Using your imagination to shape your future can be a very powerful projection, yet it is static. Writing it down is even more powerful, though it is more like sending out a signal of a black and white movie. However, drawing it out using coloured felt pens and writing down words of how you will feel when it materialises is like sending a full colour movie out to the universe. This is bound to get a response sooner or later. When you are satisfied with your drawing, date it and hang it on your wall where you can see it daily.

It really does not matter whether you draw well or not, but just make sure you choose wisely what you put down because you will get what you ask for, especially if it for the benefit of others! Remember, if what you dream of is linked to shining your light, this is one of the greatest contributions you can make to humanity. Also, as a word of caution: without clearing out the garden of your mind, visualising your future will simply remain 'wishful thinking' because limiting beliefs, phobias and guilt will block the flow.

PRACTICE #5

Self-influence towards authenticity – Visualisation

You cannot change your past, yet your future is determined by what you will think in the NOW! So, you can start exercising the 'muscles' of your imagination to make your dreams come true by practicing visualisation. It is a well-known method used by Olympic champions during their training. Find a quiet place, close your eyes and follow the instructions below:

1. Only practice this once a day.
2. And only for about five to ten minutes each time. Do not become obsessed with it.
3. Imagine every detail of your dream – visual imagery, sounds, colours, smells.
4. And, most importantly, FEEL the feelings you would like to feel if your dream came true.
5. If you haven't already, put yourself in the picture.
6. Imagine the end result (do not worry about HOW exactly it will happen). Allow for every possibility!
7. Express gratitude for it becoming a reality, as if it has already happened.

It is the time you have wasted for your rose that makes your rose so important.

Antoine de Saint-Exupéry, *The Little Prince*

References and Further Reading

Amma (Sri Mata Amritanandamayi Devi), (2011), *Nectar of Wisdom*, Mata Amritanandamayi Mission Trust, Kerala, India.

Antonelli, M., Donelli, D., Carlone, L., Maggini, V., Firenzuoli, F., and Bedeschi, E. (2022). Effects of forest bathing (shinrin-yoku) on individual well-being: An umbrella review. *Int. J. Environ. health Res.* 32 (8), p.p. 1842–1867.

Braden, G. (2015), *Resilience from the Heart: The Power to Thrive in Life's Extremes*, Hay House Inc., US.

Brown, B. (2015), *Daring Greatly: How the Courage to Be Vulnerable Transforms the Way We Live, Love, Parent, and Lead*, Penguin Life, US.

Clancy A.L., and Binkert J. (2017), "Accessing the Inner Self: Beliefs", in *Pivoting*, Palgrave Macmillan, NY, US, pp.73-88.

Csikszentmihalyi, M., (2008), *Flow: The Psychology of Optimal Experience*, Harper Perennial Modern Classics.

Chopra, D. (2015), *Quantum Healing*, Bantam Books Publishers, NY, US.

De Saint-Exupéry, A. (1990), *The Little Prince*

Eddy, M. (2016). *Mindful Movement: The Evolution of the Somatic Arts and Conscious Action*, Intellect Books, Bristol, UK.

Elston, T. (2019), *The NOW state®*, NLP World, UK.

Elston, T. (2010), *Knowing NLP: The real understanding of it*, NLP World, UK.

Enders, G. (2015), *The Gut*, Scribe Publications, UK.

Fogg, B.J., 2019. *Tiny habits: The small changes that change everything.* Eamon Dolan Books.

Foster, S. and Little, M. (1988), *The Book of the Vision Quest*, Prentice Hall.

Hayward, J. (1997), *Letters to Vanessa*, Shambhala Publications, Inc., US.

McEwan, K., Giles, D., Clarke, F.J., Kotera, Y., Evans, G., Terebenina, O., Minou, L., Teeling, C., Basran, J., Wood, W. and Weil, D., 2021. A pragmatic controlled trial of forest bathing compared with compassionate mind training in the UK: Impacts on self-reported wellbeing and heart rate variability. *Sustainability*, *13* (3), p.1380.

Lipton, B. (2005), *Biology of Belief*, Hay House Inc., US.

Ouspensky, P.D., (1965), *In Search of the Miraculous*, NY, Harcourt Brace Jovanovich.

Sakyong Mipham, (2003), *Turning the Mind into an Ally*, Riverhead Books, NY, US.

CHAPTER 3

Your Truth, Your Wisdom

Self-Compassion –
The Missing Link to Self-Leadership

As often mentioned in this book, we are living in the 'Age of Meeting Ourselves Again', so eyes need to be first looking inwards and then outwards. Correspondingly, in the first chapter we highlighted that the linchpin of the HEART-led model of compassionate leadership is *self-compassion*, especially when it comes to self-exploration. What appears to be stopping us from bringing out our innate basic goodness and being compassionate towards others is our wrong view of what 'self-love' means, and the 'self-aggression' we direct towards ourselves when we make mistakes. If we were full of true, unconditional love for ourselves, then our basic need for self-care would be fulfilled. In this way, we would not be consciously, or even subconsciously, looking for happiness and fulfillment outside of ourselves. Our outpouring of generosity and kindness towards others would come naturally, spontaneously, without effort, without fatigue, 'without object', or, more importantly, without expecting something in return.

Before we are in a position to 'Speak and Live our Truth', we need to have decided to diligently follow a path which ends in obtaining uninterrupted access to our truth, our wisdom, our self (*Atma*). It may seem an impossible goal. Nevertheless, as with all spiritual journeys, it is the *dedication* that you put into walking the path which places you in a powerful, self-confident position to trust your truth, and speak it out loud, not the *achievement* of the actual goal. It is the journey that matters, not the destination. On the way there, you will often encounter moments where you get glimpses of your wisdom. And, as you raise your vibration and journey upwards on your spiral of evolution, the more often you will connect to your wisdom, and the more peaceful and blissful you will feel, because your happiness will not depend on others, or the circumstances of your life. Happiness will come from within.

Our happiness is our own decision.

Amma

It is therefore *only* from a position of peace and bliss that we can speak to be heard. When being in this position, we feel just like the mountain in the 'Four Pebbles Meditation' practiced earlier – we feel steady, with strong roots. Nothing can shake us. When grounded as a mountain, our voice of truth will be coming from our *heart's wisdom*.

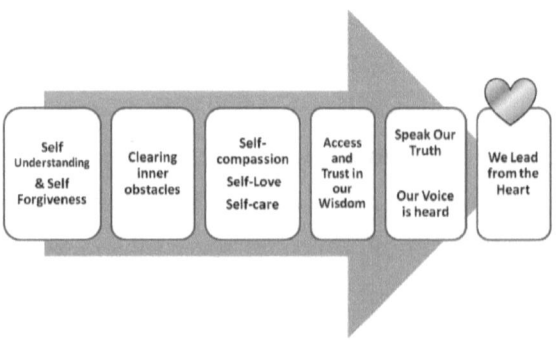

Pathway to speaking our truth: Living and leading from the heart

The access to our self is often obstructed by feelings of guilt, anger, jealousy and expectations of life and of others. Essentially, we need to venture mindfully towards embracing our shadow-self, or, as suggested earlier, to start seeing and clearing the dark corners of our unconscious mind – our limitations, constraints and negative feelings.

Only from a position of peace and bliss we can speak to be heard.

I would therefore like to dedicate this chapter to sharing with you some pathways for nurturing self-compassion and for building trust in your own wisdom. Additionally, I will be introducing some ideas that will contribute towards an improved heart-mind-body coherence and a more balanced, grounded attitude. The current chapter will be addressing the first four boxes as described in the image above, and the next chapter will be discussing the fifth box.

So, let us start this section's journey by revisiting the notion, or rather *feeling*, of 'compassion' and compare it to 'over-caring'. Then we can gain a better insight of what self-compassion and self-love is.

Compassion and Over-Caring

A few years ago, I was travelling to the UK to be trained in the 'Way of Council', a ceremony and a philosophy of human communication based on listening and talking from the heart, where people normally sit in a circle and use a 'talking piece'. During the four-hour flight, whilst sitting next to a Catholic nun, I experienced an epiphany. Dressed all in white and with a friendly composition, she encouraged me to ask her questions. I found out to my amazement and delight that she had held many talking circles during her work of service.

She said the most challenging circles of all had been to alleviate the hatred amongst Palestinian and Jewish adolescents.

I asked her what was the way into the heart and how could she possibly help them feel the pain of their enemy? Her response was not what I expected. 'The way in is through "logic", through the mind and its capacity for cognition,' she said. Firstly, she explained that you need to get them to understand what it is like to be in the other's shoes. Then, through this understanding, the mind would inform the heart, and they would then be in a position to go beyond simply perceiving the other's pain. They would also be able to *feel* the other's pain and maybe even reach as far as to forgive them, and to wish deeply that their suffering will be alleviated. This was, for me, a brilliant example of the unfolding of the mysteries of the 'mind-heart partnership'.

'Compassion' was also discussed in the first chapter. Here, however, we need to briefly revisit it in order to see its difference from 'over-caring', and how 'compassion' and 'self-compassion' share the same facets. We have already mentioned compassion's three facets: 1) perceiving the pain of another and seeing the situation as it *really* is; 2) *briefly* feeling the pain of another; 3) *discerning* what is most needed by the sufferer in order to alleviate their pain. It may seem like a three-staged process, but they take place in a seamless fashion.

The three italicised words in these facets of 'compassion', if misunderstood or overlooked, can have devastating effects on both ourselves and on the others that receive it. Firstly, we will examine the word 'briefly'. Without an attitude of 'touch and go', of feeling the pain of the other, we can easily lower our vibration to such a degree that we cannot be of any help to the other person. So, by simply becoming overly sympathetic to the pain of another, we not only go into the other person's shoes but we also weld our feet in their shoes, unable to step out of them again and swing into action.

Becoming helpless and drained of energy are limits which can be easily reached if we allow ourselves to be constantly bombarded by the world news that the media feeds us, because it only focuses on negative events and deeds. The suffering of the world will most certainly not be alleviated if we perpetually worry about it. We can remain aware of it, send a silent prayer to the sufferers, and then take action in alleviating the pain of those that need our help in our immediate or close surroundings, physical or virtual. Quality is always more impactful than quantity. In other words, it is better to help one human being in a generous and meaningful way rather than help many, hastily. Usually, people simply need our time and ears. They would rather be heard, than be given material goods.

And here is a revolutionary idea that you might frown upon. I do so myself when I'm out of balance and in 'I'm here to save the world' mode. We forget that our impact in 'doing good' can be magnified, simply by helping ourselves to release, let go, relax, to not do, and celebrate life more. Sipping on a mug of hot chocolate or treating ourselves to a scoop of the world famous 'Joe's'* vanilla ice cream may prove more beneficial to the people surrounding us than we think.

The other two italicised words in compassion's three facets are: 'really' seeing the situation as it is, and 'discernment'. Both words are connected to our ability of clear thinking, foresight and intuition. In this context, I have personally had close encounters with these two words myself since they are key to curing one of my neuroses, which is my habit of offering unsolicited advice. Yes, of course I have many excuses for it: 'I'm a teacher', 'I'm a parent', etc. However, the damage done by removing the lessons that another person may need to get from a challenging situation in order for them to evolve may be significant.

---

* Joe's Ice Cream is a brand of ice cream that was first launched at the little town of Mumbles, right next to my birthplace Swansea in Wales, UK and is by most accounts heavenly to taste, and now, widely distributed and world renowned.

Empower others by allowing them to take on responsibility of themselves and find their own solutions!

In addition to this, I have found that another helpful guideline on practicing discernment when deciding what compassionate action to take, if any, is the answer to this question: 'How do I best utilise my energy to be of service to others?' A word of caution here! I'm not suggesting that we cease to be spontaneous and authentic in our compassionate practice. By all means, if we see a stranger in need of shelter or food, we should do whatever we impulsively feel like doing without a second thought. I'm referring to circumstances whereby the person receiving our compassion does not seem to be alleviated from their suffering because, in actual fact, they are feeding off it. For example, a middle-aged woman who is ill in bed for months on end and who could contribute towards her healing but subconsciously chooses not to make an effort because she enjoys the constant attention and care she is getting from her partner. 'Discernment' will reappear again as a notion in the section on time management.

On a final note, the cases highlighted above all fall under the category of 'over-care' and are not helpful reactions to other people's suffering – neither for us as givers of care, nor for the others as its receivers. Doc Childer, HeartMath founder, refers to over-care, or worrying about others, as 'One of our mind's favourite hangouts when our vibes are low' – in other words, when we ourselves are in a negative emotional state.

We will soon discover that 'self-compassion' has, just like 'compassion', three aspects to it as well. Only, of course, with 'self-compassion' the giver and the receiver is ourself.

Ego, Awareness and Humility

Spiritual teacher Anita Moorjani was brought up in India in a culture where, more so than in the West, young girls are taught to remain silent and obedient. Any signs of non-conformity or disagreement are regarded as disrespectful, unthoughtful actions (or words), driven by their ego and sometimes disgraceful for the whole family. Many religions posit that humility is achieved by shattering our ego. Through such cultural imprints, the feminine energy of being sensitive to others' needs, and the collective unconscious stereotyping of a woman's role in society, drives many women to feel that they need to keep apologising for taking up space on the planet. Think back on how many times *you* might have apologised for something that was not your fault in the first place.

After having a near-death experience with a cancer diagnosis, Anita had a revelation and grasped how important the ego is in helping us mature and take charge of our life. She realised that she could not blame her cancer on God, or the doctors, or her family. She needed to self-lead herself into healing. Since then, she has become one of the most important advocates of women, in particular by raising their ego, and here I will share with you some of her teachings, which may place the ego under a different light to what you are used to. So, remember to remain open-minded!

She maintains that the confusion arises from our experience of people with a 'Big' ego. We then think that having an ego and expressing our needs is negative and rebuked as being 'ego-centric'. Sadly, we shut our light off and just get on with the business of taking care of our kids, the household, the family and extended family, and our boss at work. We neglect our own needs and set fire to our dreams. As a result, we suffer from over-exhaustion and develop many mental and physical ailments, then become a burden rather than being of service to others.

When you ignore your soul's calling, it will never give up chasing you, and eventually it will catch up with you!

In contrast, we nurture a healthy ego when we show ourselves self-compassion, self-love and self-care. When we gently embrace our *shadow* and appreciate our unique talents, we are confidently rooted in the ground and feel blessed and protected. We inhabit our true authentic self, where our heart is. From this place of self-leadership, we can competently and compassionately lead others.

The counterbalance of an inflated ego, according to Anita, is 'awareness': being aware of our connection to everybody else. So, when our ego is as raised as our awareness, we feel deserving of fulfilling our dreams, our creativity unleashes itself and we welcome obtaining leadership positions to serve others. If our ego is low and our awareness is high, we put ourselves last. If our ego is high and our awareness low, we become arrogant and egocentric, and we are likely to step over others to achieve our personal goals. Finally, if both our ego and our awareness are low, then we harbour feelings of loneliness and disconnection from the world. We wear a suit of armour as our protection from human emotion. We are easy prey to addiction, and we may choose escapism as a relief to our suffering.

The issue of humility does not arise when ego and awareness are in balance because 'presence' is part of being 'aware'. It means being 'awake' in a world of suffering where cooperation is required, not up in a ego-trip cloud thinking the world awaits your arrival to be saved! Humility means that you totally appreciate that you are *the conduit* through which divine creativity will manifest and, in actual fact, that your name or title does not matter. The credit, however, which does go out to you is that you agreed with your own free will to become this conduit – because you *do* have a choice whether to accept the 'job' or not. To this end, a compassionate leader is also one that displays gentleness, subtleness, equanimity and humility.

> **Humility means that you totally appreciate that you are the conduit through which divine creativity will manifest and, in actual fact, that your name or title does not matter.**

Ultimately, the need for balance in the relationship of ego and awareness reflects the need for balance between our masculine and feminine energies, irrespective of gender. Many women find it hard to embrace their ego. Their dominant energy remains their feminine one. On the other hand, there are other women that adopt masculine, patriarchal stereotypes, particularly in the workplace. Their energy is infused by aggression and superiority, and they are often first-class tyrants. It is likely that a larger number of women would wish to become leaders if they managed the balance of their own masculine–female energies more effectively.

Self-Forgiveness

The act of 'forgiving' has been one of my personal quests. In the past, I have found it hard to do in the first place and, when I thought I had forgiven the other, the universe would test me and I would fail because the pain was still there. On the reverse side of asking for forgiveness, I would often hurriedly utter, 'I'm sorry' and then, a few weeks later, I would repeat the same habitual pattern. My Greek Christian Orthodox background has made matters even worse since there seems to be no explanation as to how exactly 'forgiveness' takes place. By not truly forgiving, and not being capable of asking for forgiveness in a meaningful way, we go around carrying negative feelings of anger and bitterness, not only towards the one that acted in a seemingly 'unforgiving' way, but also towards ourselves for allowing ourselves to be victimised. We create our own prison and bake on our own fire of angry flames. What a waste of energy!

A leader can only be compassionate when they are free. Freedom comes from knowing how to truly forgive and ask for forgiveness. And these acts take large doses of humility.

In his book *Resilience from the Heart*, scientist and spiritual teacher Gregg Braden maintains that the key to personal transformation is to cultivate '*Resilience*', meaning to develop the capacity to heal unresolved pain. The change happens literally in our heart organ, rather than through the re-wiring of our brain. The increase in deaths through heart disease is astonishing. He explains that this is due to the drop in people's heart rate variability (HRV). If, as we grow older, we get imprisoned by our limiting beliefs and do not practice forgiveness, the specific changes in time (or variability) between successive heart beats becomes more 'locked' into a regular pattern, so our body is less resilient to stress. We therefore have less overall resilience to what life throws at us.

Such a significant gap in knowledge about the immeasurable value of practicing forgiveness also has a detrimental effect on our ability to practice self-forgiveness and, therefore, self-compassion. We cannot possibly take charge of our life and become leaders of others unless our own unconscious cupboard is clear of feelings of remorse, or disappointment for past decisions or acts we undertook.

In my search for a way, I came across a suggestion by one of my Greek spiritual teachers, Pegki Christofi, which also illuminates the beauty of the mind-heart partnership. In her book, *Imprints*, she explains that the measure of whether forgiveness was effective or not is made visible by the virtuous acts and positive behavior that we, the 'victims', engage in after the undertaking of forgiveness. A sure sign of true forgiveness is if we no longer feel pain when meeting or thinking of the person that acted in an ignorant way.

In preparation for such control over our possibly immature ego, we first need to get used to the idea of 'non-judgment'. It is the act that can be judged and not the performer of the act. Also, in Greek the verb to 'forgive' is 'συγχωρώ', which literally means 'to get into the same space as the one that has acted ignorantly', with the intention to unite with them. Such a change in viewpoint can (as mentioned in the section on compassion) have a miraculous effect on our insight of the performer's circumstances.

With these two understandings in mind, we could first practice what she calls a 'Release'. This gives us back our precious freedom and gives a chance to the performer of the deed to also feel free from having to beg for our forgiveness. We release the performer from any obligation or debt, and we release our trapped negative perception of the related experience. The key here is that we release because we are truly willing to do so and not because of some moral obligation. What follows now are the steps we can take to practice 'Release'.

This practice also has elements of 'Time-Based Techniques' and neuro-linguistic programming. Moreover, this practice can be used for the purposes of releasing our own feelings of guilt for something we did or did not do, said or did not say. For instance, the perception of not having spent enough time, or shown enough love, to one of our beloveds who is now dead haunts many people. In such a case, the performer of the act would be *ourselves* instead of someone else. And we would try to 'walk in the shoes' of our past self in order to self-forgive.

PRACTICE #6
Self-exploration & self-influence towards authenticity – From 'release' to 'forgiveness' and 'self-forgiveness'

Warning! This is not to be attempted for extremely traumatic life events. In such cases, you are advised to seek professional advice and help.

1. **Focus on the NOW:** Find a quiet spot and, alone, do a focusing exercise (e.g., five minutes of balancing your breath and mindfulness meditation).
2. **Improve perception:** Next, imagine that you are 'floating' back over your timeline into the past and that you are hovering over the event as an observer. It is important to keep this attitude while doing so, as it keeps our mind awake in the present and protects us from the pain of the past, allowing us to be non-judgmental and openly

curious about how each person may have perceived what was happening. At this point, it is an opportunity to see what it feels like 'walking in the other person's shoes' when the event occurred.

3. **Understand the lessons:** While still 'floating' above the event, try to see if your current, present day, more mature and wise self can discern the lessons from such a challenging situation. The lessons are the real 'diamonds' of any seemingly unfortunate or distressing event in our life, and these, when we 'get them', transform us into true life warriors. If, however, you find this step difficult to do, be gentle towards yourself and try this whole practice again when you are ready and willing to simply observe the event and be more honest about your own share of the outcome.

4. **Integrate the lessons:** Understanding the lessons from an event involving another person is less than half the journey if these are not integrated in our current life. You can do this at a mental and an emotional level by running through an example of how you would react in a similar circumstance in the present moment. This new mode of operation will hopefully change your own limiting behavior, as there are always two sides to a dissonant act or relationship.

5. **Accept:** The act of acceptance is both a mental and a heart-based action. You try to accept at both levels the actions of the performer and your own share of the dissonance.

6. **Release:** By this stage, and if you are still really willing, the release of any ill-feelings, pain, or need for redemp-

tion or punishment will take place almost effortlessly. Nevertheless, action is better than thoughts, so writing down words of release will 'cement' the agreement you have made with yourself. These writings do not need to be shared with the other person. If you have been sincere in this process, the words of release will be reflected in your future deeds. Here, Pegki suggests that this practice of writing needs to be repeated three times over a period of three weeks, at the same day and time – the purpose is to demonstrate your willingness. Let us assume that the person we are trying to forgive is named Maria. An example of the words would be: *'Let all dissonant energy that exists between Maria and I be released into the light. Maria is free from me, and I am free from Maria. I am free from you. You are free from me. Thank you for the experience.'*

Source: this practice is an adaptation from the teachings and book of Pegki Christofi, "Imprints" (in Greek Αποτυπώματα), SOL Publications, Athens, Greece, pp. 34-38, (www.faroshelp.gr), and also combines elements of 'Time-Based Techniques' and Neuro-Linguistic Programming.

As discussed, a poor understanding of the act of forgiveness means that we also lack the ability to free ourself from guilt for past actions. Self-forgiveness is, from my experience, the second stumbling block to becoming a compassionate leader (the first one being a poor understanding of the difference between using your ego as the driving force towards authentic self-expression and being egocentric).

Self-Compassion

Below are some guidelines to help you cultivate self-compassion.

Knowing your needs and desires

As humans, we have needs, wishes and desires. These are the ego's 'children' and it is healthy to recognise that we have them and express them, as long as they do not turn into badly behaved children and become aggressively passionate about being satisfied. This is when the ego 'overruns' our awareness of others around us, as discussed a little earlier.

Needs and wishes tend to be about what we need in the present, or an accumulation of past longings, whereas desires tend to be more future-based and are often related to our soul's calling, dreams and visions. We may notice a close connection between our needs and desires and our life values. Caring about our needs, wishes and desires generates the vital energy we require to feel in harmony and remain in life's flow. These may be as simple as our need to communicate with another human being, our need to take a break and spend a day by the sea, our wish to experience the Aura Borealis in the Arctic, or as complex as building an alternative school or planting a whole forest, just like Jadav 'Molai' Payeng did in India.

The American film *Runaway Bride* starring Julia Roberts is a useful reminder of how regenerative it is to make sure we care for our needs and fulfil our dreams. Julia impersonates a young woman who could not decide on a partner, so every time she arrived at the church to get married, she would change her mind at the very last minute, leaving behind mayhem and a bewildered, disappointed future bridegroom. The reason for this was that she had no idea about what her needs and desires were, even the most basic ones, such as what her favourite colour or favourite food was. By not knowing and not satisfying our longings, we may find ourselves confused in our own maze, often making reckless decisions on critical life junctures, such as the choice of a partner, and then finding ourselves trapped at dead-end or challenging life paths.

I have found that many women have difficulty in deciding whether they want, or do not want, something. I know from first-hand experience that, in the past, it has been even more difficult for me to communicate to others that I did not want to do something. I would seldom say 'No', and, if I did utter the two letter word, I would use a whisper of a voice, then proceed to apologise profusely and feel I needed to justify my refusal. The result of such self-aggression would be that I would feel I had allowed others to exceed my limits, and a sense of self-betrayal would run through my body, ending up with the sensation of being punched in the stomach (trapped anger). Do you relate to this 'stickiness'?

In turn, as we will see in the following chapter, knowing our desires but not expressing them clearly, or at all, not only stifles our creativity but also attracts us towards difficult life paths and creates dysfunctional relationships. So, what steps would be useful to take towards training ourselves in identifying our needs?

Firstly, silently practicing self-awareness and non-judgmental observation without the use of negative, critical self-talk. By doing this mindfully, we learn to become curious and sincere about how we feel in the present moment. What are our emotions and what are our related bodily feelings? And knowing that it is 'OK' to be angry, it is 'OK' to be sad, it is 'OK' to feel lonely is important. These are universal human feelings! Catching our breath in the midst of our chaotic daily life every now and then might prove invaluable. The following three practices will aid you in managing self-talk, exploring your deepest wishes and igniting your creative spark.

> **Try next time you make a mistake throwing your hands up in the air and saying with excitement and curiosity, 'How fascinating!'**
>
> Benjamin Zander, expert on motivational leadership, former conductor of the Boston Philharmonic Orchestra

PRACTICE #7
Self-influence towards authenticity – 'Self-talk' and small paper bags

For this practice you will need two small paper bags, some coloured markers and a twenty-minute break from phones, children and work.

Draw a face on both paper bags. One will be a joyful and sweet-looking face, and the other will be a wild and angry face. Next, place them on your hands. You will be playing puppet theatre!

This is a self-observation exercise, so it will be good if you observe your feelings and reactions without self-judgment – be spontaneous!

So, first the 'wild and angry' paper bag talks to you: it tells you off and criticises you about something you recently did or said. Perhaps you recognise this monologue. The 'sweet and happy' paper bag kindly waits for the wild bag to stop. But, because it may take its time, give it three minutes.

The 'sweet and happy' bag takes its turn and now speaks to you gently. Imagine it is your best friend: how would he or she speak to you, in order to alleviate you from the guilt and to soften the harsh criticism given to you by the wild and angry paper bag? Perhaps it would say, 'It is only human to make mistakes', or 'You were particularly tired on that occasion, so you were not aware of your actions', or 'You had your mind elsewhere and did not respect the needs of the other person', or 'Other times you handle similar situations much better and you need patience and practice to learn a new behaviour.'

You may need to repeat the exercise until the 'sweet' paper bag talks for more time than the 'wild' one! This practice will help you become more aware of the aggressive self-talk you often engage in. Research by behavioural psychologists has proven that our behaviour does not improve when we speak strictly to ourselves. In fact, it creates a greater disconnect from our inner world.

And, of course, as we have already seen, when we do not treat ourselves with love, patience, and compassion, we cannot offer these gifts to others.

So, I invite you to practice becoming the 'sweet' paper bag towards yourself and not the 'wild' paper bag towards others!

PRACTICE # 8
Self-exploration – A daily expression of self-love

When you are unsure of what your deepest wishes or your most basic needs are, a quick practice to identify them would be to make a note of five wishes in your beautiful notebook. Allow for whatever comes to mind, without self-criticism. Write down beside each wish at least two corresponding emotions that you imagine feeling when you satisfy these wishes.

You can make the whole practice more playful if, instead of writing down your wishes using words, you create a collage of images representing your wishes and then make a note with a coloured felt tip pen of the corresponding emotions next to each picture.

PRACTICE #9
Self-Influence towards authenticity – A daily expression of self-love

A question that you can ask yourself on a daily basis as a practice is:

'If you did love yourself, what would you be creating?'

This is a healthy alternative to judging yourself when you are not showing self-care.

(Source: Anita Moorjani's 2017 interview on 'Wisdom from the North' YouTube channel. The interview title: 'The Real Truths, Self-love, Ego and Fear')

EXERCISE #13

Self-exploration - Do you show yourself enough self-compassion?

This is a quick self-check to alert you as to how gentle and loving you are towards yourself when each of the following situations occur. Place the corresponding number next to each question, depending on your recent average experience:

1 = never; 2 = seldom; 3 = sometimes, 4 = most times, 5 = always.

Try to complete the test within one minute.

When I make a mistake, I keep reprimanding myself repeatedly and feel guilty or angry about my behaviour.
When I'm going through a stressful period, I pressurise myself to keep going.
When I'm feeling sad, I keep focusing on all that seems to be going wrong with my life or on the 'things' that I do not have.

> I generally feel cut off from the rest of the world, as if I cannot find my own tribe.
>
> I often admire other people, and in conversations I keep referring to them.
>
> The lower your total score, the more compassionate you are towards yourself and more connected to your true self and your inner wisdom. So, the lowest score of 5 corresponds to a very high level of self-compassion and the highest score of 25 corresponds to a very low level of self-compassion.
>
> Bear in mind that when 'all is going well' in our life, it may feel easy to be caring towards ourselves. It is especially important to develop self-love habits so that we continue to show self-compassion even during highly distressing periods or times of mental and bodily exhaustion. After all, these are when we need self-love the most.
>
> Remember not to rush into judging yourself if your score was high. Simply observe, be gentle with YOU and curious as to why this might be happening.
>
> Such an approach is often all that is needed to 'shift things' inside.

Time Management – How to be Stress Free

My Uncle Manolis was almost ninety at the time of this episode in my life. He was one of seven children brought up in a village under snowy mountains on the island of Crete. During our country's occupation, he spent two of his teenage years as one of the 1,500 youngsters building the airport of Tymbaki in the centre of Crete, in conditions that would be hard to imagine these days. Courageous and polite, yet cheeky at times, and full of life, as a young man he used to love dancing the waltz in the village hall with his only sister. This was before he married. His wife died before him, and he was very sad. He used to speak to me about his early years with nostalgia, so a little while before he died, I made him a promise. The two siblings would be reunited and dance the waltz again.

I remember how I kept putting it off for weeks on end because there was always some other, more important situation or emergency taking priority. Until finally, my inner voice became too loud for me to ignore: 'What are you waiting for? How much longer do you think he will live?' Fortunately, I did finally listen. Two days later, he was admitted to hospital for the final time. I wonder how many similar stories could we share?

Believing that stress comes from time pressures is a frequent misconception, since we all have been given an equal amount of time to spend each day. So, why is it that some are less stressed than others? Is it because their physiology is more resilient to life's pressures, or is it because they have chosen to have a less responsible job, or chosen to have no children? I have noticed how people suffer from choices they make when they do not allow for space in their hectic daily schedules. These people look drained of hope and run around like rats chasing their tails in the tunnel of life. If you asked them, 'Are you happy with your life?' they would respond, 'Yes, of course! But . . .' And there is always something missing.

Being increasingly curious about why some people get ill from stress and why others are joyfully stress free, I systematically started to interview stress-free people to discover their secret. They all had one thing in common. They were all passionate about what they did on a daily basis, which gave meaning to their lives. They felt their life had a purpose. Being less stressed, therefore, is not about being more efficient with time because, even if we had a spare moment, we would still automatically replace the space by responding to one more email. It is neither about being better 'planners' nor 'to-do listers' because the stress will still be there, even if we 'juggle all our balls' in the air better. And, of course, there will always be unexpected events that will derail our plans.

Many of us use our smartphones to wake us up, to remind us when to drink water, or to be notified when a new email has popped into our inbox. We believe that, if we save time, *then* we will get to enroll in the evening class to learn a new language, or *then* we will take our elderly parents on a trip. The mentality is that, if we save time, we will be able to create a better life. We, therefore, defer the NOW for tomorrow, postponing our happiness. What this special creed of people that I interviewed had in common was that they had *invested* time in building a life that made them happy, and then time was no longer an issue. Their mantra was: 'Build a fulfilling, happy life by saving time.' Not the other way around!

Yet another misconception about time comes from Newtonian physics, which asserts that our given time of twenty-hour hours cannot increase. There will always be 1,440 minutes and 86,400 seconds in a day. Nonetheless, infused by the power of our thoughts and emotions, time can become expansive. For example, while waiting for our lover's train to arrive, time seems to have stopped, whereas when we are rushing through the airport to catch our plane that is just about to take off, every second counts.

In the second chapter, we demonstrated the importance of identifying our key life values. These act as a 'daily compass' which keeps guiding us to what is closer to our calling. In this section, I would like to introduce you to another way of thinking about time. Instead of breaking it up in hours and minutes, you may adopt the 'three circles of time' perspective.

A recent survey I carried out about female executives in European cybersecurity gives us a picture of how they use their time in an average week. They had a choice as to how they would invest their time for all three circles (see image below). Likewise, assuming we dedicate fifty hours to our work, we can decide how we allocate the remainder of the sixty-eight hours left, since a leader has no 'obligations', as such. Everything we choose to do, we do with joy and presence, not because we are obliged by some external force to do so. This serves as a reminder of chapter two's conclusion that 'our thoughts make our reality'.

Average time expenditure in a week of a busy Cybersecurity female executive...

Total weekly time = 168 hours of which:

50 hours are for working

50 hours are for sleeping

This allows for 68 hours of

'FREE' time per week!

So, the *circle of time for our family and friends* may also be used for volunteering. This circle is our source of intimacy, care, compassion, love and feeling loved, and that we belong. When we cultivate resonant relationships, it induces positive emotional states. These activities nourish our heart and our relationships with others. The family and friends time circle is a source of 'Heart Vitamin', as I prefer to call it.

The *personal time circle* is the time we take out to be on our own, in peace, without outside voices. It is a quiet time to help us listen to our needs and desires – the time to dream of the future and how we could use our talents in a better way. We women are so much more than our jobs, our children's mother, our partner's partner, a daughter, or a sister! Virginia Wolf once said: 'A woman must have money and a room of her own if she is to write. This, I have come to believe, applies to us even if we do not take to writing. Creativity is the driving force of any woman. The 'room of our own' does not have to be a physical one. It simply needs to be a private space without any interference: no smartphones, no watches, no children.

Choosing your 'power place' in nature is always a good choice. Personal time can be jogging in the park, going to a movie on your own, journaling over a cup of coffee, meditating, or even simply sitting in your very own armchair before going to bed and reading a page of your favourite book. The personal time circle is what fuels our creativity. It helps us to develop panoramic vision, explore more choices, think more strategically, solve problems and even be less reactive to our emotions. So, like the family and friends time circle, this too develops our 'heart's brain', but this time not in relation to others but to what we need at the deepest, unconscious level. I call the personal time circle the source of our 'Chi Vitamin' or 'Prana Vitamin'.

Keeping a close eye on these three time circles, we can become more aware of self-created imbalances in our life. When we slip into the habit of allowing the time we spend in work to by far exceed the time we spend with our friends and family, and we also invest very little time for our personal space, we then get frustrated. We easily lose patience and often feel that people treat us with injustice, and that others are making our life harder. We lose our humour, our lightness, our humanity. We become overly goal-oriented – only brain and no heart. I recognise this feeling well, since this is how I was when I started working in the corporate world at the beginning of my working life.

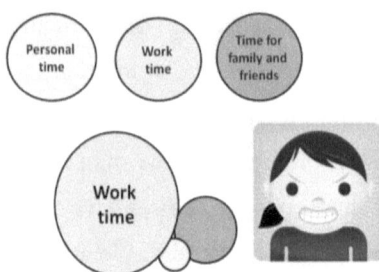

We can also quite easily get out of balance when we become overly focused on being with our young children, caring for an ill parent or constantly volunteering. Then, although it is in our nature to care for others, after a while this is not fulfilling enough.

Of course, if we also hold a day job as well as caring for others, we soon start to feel stressed, as if our day is divided into two: family and work. We hardly recognise that, somewhere in between, is our 'little me' crying out for attention, and that when this situation is prolonged we fall into depression. We feel unloved, we eat and dress poorly and we feel like a 'doormat'. This is when alarm bells should go off because, as discussed many times in this book, you cannot be compassionate towards others if you do not show any compassion towards yourself.

Even though it is hard to keep these circles in balance, you may wish to use them as a blueprint for what being in balance means: the three circles, almost equal in size, are not of course based on the quantity of time but on the quality of time spent remaining in the flow in all three occasions.

On one final note, notice how in both cases of imbalance the one circle that always gets squashed down is the personal time circle. We so easily forget that it is during our private moments we get to exercise our inner wisdom and muscles of intuition. As previously discussed, scientific research has proven that our heart has an intelligence of its own and that it sends signals to the brain to help us make more informed choices. It is the soft whisper of our heart's voice, which might warn us of a car heading our way around a blind bend, or tell us not to take that job even though it pays well.

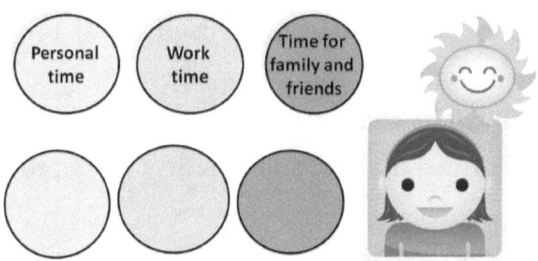

One of the biggest sources of stress is when our mind says something different to our heart. By systematically squashing down the personal time circle, we keep having a loud noise around us which stops us from listening to our inner guide – we do not allow for things to unfold, and we have no idea what our desires are. However, know that we as women are resilient and, even if we lose balance, when we rest and focus, we do become younger and recover our energy! As Clarissa Pinkola Estes, the author of *Women Who Run With the Wolves*, mentions: 'The circle of women [. . .] always closes to fill in for those who go on rest leave.'

> **If you've lost focus, just sit down and be still. Take the idea and rock it to and fro. Keep some of it and throw some away, and it will renew itself. You need do no more.**
>
> Clarissa Pinkola Estes

The great paradox of these three circles is that, when the circle of personal time is at its fullest size, then it becomes the fuel for the other two circles and, as if by magic, our time multiplies!

The exercise that follows offers a practical tool to explore which types of activities you personally spend your time on. In this way, you will be able to detect any imbalances, whether you make good time investments, and to reflect on improvements you could make.

EXERCISE #14

Self-Influence towards authenticity – The three circles of time

Normally, we all have a general idea of how we spend our time in an average week. This perception depends on our ability to prioritise and to say 'No', our stage in life, our workload, our family status, our beliefs, our values, and many more.

It is only when we actually put pen to paper and focus on mapping our weekly activities that we realise how we could improve on our Return on Time Invested (ROTI).

In this exercise, you will be asked to map your weekly activities, based on the 'three circles of time' categories, to record the length of time these activities take and to assess their contribution towards building a better future for yourself and those around you. And remember, it is not so much about managing time in order to stretch it out, because no matter what your workload is or how many children you have, we all have the exact same amount of time in a day: twenty-four hours! Reducing your stress levels is more about improving on your ROTI.

Practicalities: although the template for you to do the mapping will be provided here, it is highly recommended that you steer away from computers and do this assessment the old-fashioned way, needing no more than a large sheet of paper, a pencil, a rubber, two highlighter pens and a couple of coloured felt tip pens, or more if you feel like drawing. One final but essential detail: choose to do this exercise when you are relaxed and alone.

STAGE 1: Mapping of weekly activities

First, copy the template below onto your sheet of paper. Next, by reflecting on an average week, identify weekly activities which are not only the most time consuming but also the ones that are necessary or significant to you. Just place them under one of the three categories in the following circles of time, and be as precise and detailed as you can. Once finished, add up each column to get the total number of hours per circle/category.

Personal time		Work time		Time for family and friends	
ACTIVITIES	hours	ACTIVITIES	hours	ACTIVITIES	hours
TOTAL time		TOTAL time		TOTAL time	

STAGE 2: Identifying activities that make a contribution to a better future

Here you will need to reflect on the activities listed in all three circles/categories and mark with two different highlighter pens the ones which, if you dedicate more time, will significantly contribute towards a better future.

A/directly for you: for example, exercising regularly at least three times per week will help you to be healthy in the years to come, learning a foreign language may give your career a boost, and practicing mindful meditation will reduce your stress levels.

B/for the people around you and indirectly for you: for instance, quality time invested in spending more time with your young children, doing voluntary work or teaching something related to your skill sets in a local college, landscaping the garden of your family home to have more family gatherings.

As discussed earlier, these types of activities are the ones that gain you more time in the long run, because time invested in them now contributes to a happier life in the years ahead. If you have very few such activities, then this is a point of reflection and you may wish to add some. It would be to your benefit if there was at least one such activity for every day of your working week. Don't forget, time is not a renewable source, so invest in activities wisely and increase your ROTI!

STAGE 3: Minimizing or ceasing some of the remaining activities

Now that you have located the activities most significant to building a better future, use the felt tip pens to underline activities that: A/can be done in less time or less frequently; B/can be deleted from the list, as they don't seem that important any more; C/can be given to someone else to do, for example someone who you train and easily supervise, or, if necessary, you learn to trust.

STAGE 4: Identifying areas of imbalance

Having completed the previous stages, it will be a lot easier to identify areas of imbalance. First, notice if your three circles of time are almost equal in the total weekly hours allocated. If not, identify the activities that are the source of this imbalance. It is usual for women to have very little total time invested in personal activities. Realising the significance of personal activities and allowing sufficient time for these on a daily basis will, in the long run, lead to a healthier mental and bodily state, reduced stress and 'unknown' frustration, increased ability to think clearly, an awareness of the 'signs' and use of your intuition, and, therefore, a much higher quality of decision making and a higher degree and frequency of compassion towards others.

Next, notice whether there is a lack of activities in all three categories that will contribute towards a better future. See if you would like to add, alter or delete something on your weekly activities chart.

The exercise on 'values' in Chapter Two will act as an addition to your understanding of what is significant in your life.

And finally, you may wish to invest some extra time doing this self-assessment by picking up the remaining felt tip pens and drawing on an extra blank sheet what you would like your life to be like in five years' time.

Have fun doing it, and remember Walt Disney's famous words: 'If you can imagine it, then you can do it!'

Over the years, I have found that maintaining new helpful habits, especially those that are connected to daily prioritizing, becomes easier if I use prompts in my living work space. So, here I offer some 'relaxation mantras'. These are short sayings that I post on my walls interchangeably to help me keep living a rich, balanced life!

I invest time to build the life I want TODAY. I do not leave it for tomorrow!

I will not postpone NOW for tomorrow! If it makes me happy, I do it NOW!

The more I hurry, the less time I have!

Only I am responsible for my happiness.

I am the Director of my life!

Breath ... three deep breaths. Morning, Lunch, Bedtime.

Small hinges can make big door swings!

Little changes ... Big shifts!

'A woman must have money and a room of her own.' Virginia Wolf

Put the mask on first, then to others 'sitting' next to you!

Am I being creative?

Allow things to unfold ... do not chase – attract!

I choose to say 'NO' once in a while.

What exactly do I need right now?

Are my values being met today through my actions?

Take time out to waltz a little or ... much!!

Our Sacred Body – Allowing it to Flourish

Our body is the temple of our soul. This is true for all humans. Without this temple, our soul has no place to rest, and it departs. What would you do if you had easy access to a temple? Would you think of it as a hindrance to feeling joyful and spiritually elevated? Would you not feel protected and strong when you sit still inside it for a while? Would you not make sure there is always a candle burning on its alter?

Our body is the temple of our soul.

I began to internalise this understanding only ten years ago. Before that, I felt as if it was a heavy shell which I was obliged to carry everywhere I went, a painful burden that was often in need of 'medical repair', and a means to receive what I mistakenly thought was true love from men. How could it have been otherwise since I deeply believed, and therefore felt, that my body and soul were not related in any way? In fact, not only did I believe that they were unrelated but also that tendering to the needs of my intellect was a far better cause, and use of, my time than listening to the needs of my physical body, or, for that matter, the soft whisper of my soul's desire to free itself from my self-made reality.

The superiority of the intellect was a reflection of my cultural conditioning, one that has been around for more than 5,000 years. Its connection to the 'ego–awareness' imbalance, with the scales tipping towards 'awareness', may become obvious to you here. Others' needs always took priority over mine. If I was in any way physically ill or emotionally unstable, I felt I 'should' quick-fix it, put on a 'stiff upper lip' and just get on with life. This became a vicious circle of pushing my emotions, needs and desires into a dark closet until it was full and exploded! My story towards freedom may resonate with many of you. I'm no exception.

It is no coincidence that, once I decided to consciously work on changing my limiting beliefs and values, I 'received' my soul's calling in 2009: the vision of 'Sparkles in Young People's Eyes' and the yearning to create the 'School for Young Leaders' mentioned in the introduction. The starting point in this shift was learning to appreciate and nurture the precious 'body-mind-soul' union. I searched for teachers that taught me yoga and meditation, practices to train my scattered mind and help me become more centred. These precious guides helped me appreciate Silence and the importance of connecting within. Step by step my body started to *re-member* it was 'sacred', just like every other aspect of my being. I found it important to maintain a holistic approach when caring for my health and discovered alternative healing practices and practitioners, such as homeopathy, acupuncture and shiatsu. Not only is my body packed with more than a trillion lively cells, all with a 'mind' of their own, it is also in constant dialogue with the environment I live in, and carries imprints from my lineage and culture. Inevitably, each body is different and has different requirements.

> **'Every cell is a little sentient being. Sitting in the liver or heart or kidney, it 'knows' everything you know, but in its own fashion.'**
>
> Deepak Chopra, M.D., in *Quantum Healing*

To remain an effective leader over long periods of time requires a healthy attitude towards our body. Here, too, we need to be self-led and take full responsibility for its well-being. When we believe it is wise, we can and *should* consult the experts. However, we would fare better if *we* were the ones taking the final decision. Part of this responsibility is to continuously educate ourselves on the latest scientific and spiritual advancements relating to this beautiful gift that we were are all given: the body. Also, not forgetting collective wisdom, it is prudent to gather information from the experiences of other women. Carefully 'listening' to our body and any intuitive messages is also in our own hands. To learn the language of our body requires mindfulness and practice. And talking of practice, I have one for you right here.

PRACTICE #10
Self-influence towards authenticity – Learn to listen to your body

Practice tuning into your body, especially if you are in pain. The Body is always talking to you. It will tell you what you need to know for it to be a good servant to your soul. It will let you know what food is good for you and when you can eat it. It will speak to you in your sleep and during your rest time. It will be particularly talkative during your menses. Whatever seems to annoy you during this sacred time of the month, make sure you pay attention to it. It can be an important need that you are ignoring.

So, for this practice, switch off all electronic devices, lie on the floor or your bed and close your eyes, while focusing on your breathing. Place one hand on your chest, the other on your lower abdominal area. See if both of these areas are rising enough and to the same extent during the inhale. Try to balance the amount of air that spreads in your chest and abdomen.

Next, especially if it is in physical pain, ask your body directly, and even better the area that is in pain: 'What are you trying to tell me? What is the message you have for me?' Allow for some time to see what comes up. You can also ask it about any other aspect of your life: 'How do you feel about George as a partner?' or 'How do you feel about my job?' The response may not be in words, it might be a picture or a song that comes into your mind. It might even be in the form of a subtle feeling, a contraction or an expansion of your body. Trust the sign! Next, ask 'What do

> I need to do to make you feel more comfortable?' Again, your body will tell you. Your job is to trust the response and then ACT UPON IT!! Simple? :-)
>
> Note: When in pain, sending emerald green light to the affected area has always been one of my favourite self-healing techniques.

So, without forgetting that all are intrinsically connected, this section will cover some very basic principles of how we can develop strong temple pillars for our body. I will not profess that I'm an expert, though I enjoy learning about its intricacy, its language and amazing ability to self-heal. I will therefore lightly touch upon five of the pillars, allowing for some 'seeds' to drop: sleep, sunlight, nutrition, physical exercise and emotional health.

Sleep

Hopefully, after reading this section you will pay more attention to the quality of your sleep, if you do not already do so. Did you know that as we sleep, the brain 'cleaners' come and clean it from harmful substances? When we let them do their job well, then we help prevent degenerative brain diseases, such as Alzheimer's. Also, during our sleep, the 'service' of our organs is undertaken. Each one takes its turn. So, for example, based on Chinese medicine, our lungs are serviced between 3am and 5am. Also, at night the brain orders all that has happened to us during the previous day. After seeing all of the previous day's details, as if in a movie, it separates the important from the insignificant, identifies patterns and solves complicated problems, or gives us answers to something that we did not understand during the day that has passed.

During sleep time we capture the best ideas and, if like me, you enjoy dancing, you will learn new steps during the next night's deep-sleep phase, and not when you are actually shown them. On the other hand, in the REM (rapid eye movement) phase, whilst dreaming, our conscious, logical, critical mind sleeps, whereas the unconscious mind, which is constantly awake, will find the opportunity to 'weave' the story we say to ourselves and to others, and about who we think we are. These and more wondrous endeavors are done while we are sleeping!

When we create the right conditions for a sound sleep, one of our body's most powerful hormones is produced: 'melatonin'. Melatonin is produced by our pineal gland and operates as a neurotransmitter, sending control signals to regulate our blood pressure, the immune system, our body temperature, our reproductive organs and many other areas of our body. It is also our body's best cleaner of the cancer-causing free radicals. However, it only starts producing in the dark, after 9.30pm and peaks at approximately 1am. In fact, even a ray of light will stop the pineal gland from fully secreting it. The brain cannot distinguish between light and electromagnetic waves, so when, for example, we have our TV on in our bedroom before or during sleeping, it suppresses the production of melatonin. It is important therefore, if we use our devices all day long, to introduce a practice of gradually closing all monitors around us, ten minutes earlier, progressively every night. When our sleeping pattern is in balance, we also get our 'beauty sleep', which, according to Ayurveda practitioner Andreas Moritz, occurs for only one hour from 11pm until midnight. 'Beauty sleep' it is indeed, since it is the deepest segment of our sleep.

So guard your sleep, just like you do the rest of your health, and always have a good night's sleep before taking your most important decisions. Your first thought as you wake up is the right choice for you!

PRACTICE# 11

Self-exploration and influence towards authenticity – Just capture those dreams!

Have you ever tried to capture the dreams you have while you sleep?

According to Carl Jung, renowned psychoanalyst, dreams are an open window into the dark folds of our unconscious mind. They inform us of our fears, anxieties and deepest wishes. When you know more about what is happening inside 'there', then you can improve the quality of your life substantially. Recording them is not as difficult as it sounds, as long as you give yourself a 'command' before you fall asleep and keep a torch, a pen and paper handy by your side to record them. You may need to be patient, however, as it could take two or three nights before you manage to capture any.

Sunlight

In his book, *Heal Yourself with Sunlight*, Andreas Moritz explains that the belief that the sun causes skin cancer and aging, and that we should wear sunscreen lotions and sunglasses, is a myth. In fact, the UV rays in sunlight stimulate the thyroid gland to increase the hormone production, increasing the body's metabolic rate.

> **'The human body was designed to live outdoors, not indoors.'**
> Andreas Moritz, author and Ayurveda practitioner

Sun exposure done mindfully, and at the right hours of the day, helps our body produce cholesterol sulfate, which, combined with melatonin, synthesises vitamin D. This vitamin is vital for our health as it increases our immune system, balances cholesterol levels, and reduces the risk from arthritis, cancer and hypertension. Sunlight is a powerful detoxifier which heals our joints, dissolves mucus and, its most important benefit, makes us feel happier!

I encourage you to study how you can include sunbathing in your daily practice of self-care. If you haven't already, make the sun your best friend.

Nutrition

When I was learning how to eat as a vegetarian, my therapist and teacher, Jenni Saukkonen, taught me that it is important to maintain a balanced diet and try to eat 'all the colours of the rainbow'.

So, even with nutrition, variety remains the spice of life! Moreover, while being on a five-day fast during my 'Vision Quest', I discovered that I do not die without food, but probably would without water. This has taught me that I can experiment more, listen to my body more, and practice one or two days of fasting every month, just like they do in India, with the opportunity of *Ekadashi*, a spiritual day linked to the lunar cycle. While fasting, you not only help your body to rest from food intake, but it also shifts your consciousness to a higher vibration and helps you to reduce your attachment to it. Have you ever noticed that there are some days that you do not feel like eating, but go ahead and eat anyway because of fear of what would happen if you went without?

> **'When we recognize that we are able to eat due to the kindness of the sentient beings involved in the many activities necessary for a plate of food to arrive in front of us, attachment to food is easily replaced by gratitude toward sentient beings.'**
>
> Thubten Chodron in *The Compassionate Kitchen*

By making sure we read the labels of packaged products carefully, we take responsibility for our food intake, enabling us to reduce the amount of the three deadliest white compounds we would consume otherwise: white sugar, refined salt and white flours. If you are able, consume fresh, local, organic fruits and vegetables.

About *water* – surely there is no coincidence when we consider that the water mass on the Earth's surface is the same as in the human body, over 70 percent. So, in a way, we have an inner ocean! Based on scientific evidence gathered by Dr Emoto Masaru, every time we drink a glass of water and we say out loud that we 'love life', and then drink the water, its crystals will look like tiny, beautiful, symmetrical snowflakes and will carry into our body extremely beneficial properties and positive energy. The amount of water we need may depend on our body weight. A rough guide would be to divide our bodily weight (measured in kilos), by 30. This will give the daily amount of liters of water needed to keep our body hydrated and detoxified, depending also, of course, on the season. It is recommended that we drink 90 percent of our daily quota by 2 pm and keep one last glass of water to enjoy just before our bedtime.

'You are the ocean, not the waves that pass over you...'

Physical exercise

First and foremost, through regularly exercise we can avoid reaching 'dark nights of the soul' moments. Scientific research has proven that it has an immediate benefit on our emotional state and our ability to focus. One exercise session can significantly increase our focus for as long as two hours. In fact, we learn better after physical exercise. It will also increase our ability to react.

The positive effects are also long term. Exercise gives a great 'Return on Time Invested'. It protects our brain from neuro-degenerative diseases and reduces the speed of its defilement due to ageing, as it increases our brain's neuroplasticity. It also signals the production of strong blasts of energy which awaken our neurotransmitters into more vivid action, thus having a longer-lasting effect, increasing the continuity of our positive mood state, and decreasing the risk of cancer, even breast cancer. Christiane Northrup, M.D., claims that regular exercise can add an average of seven years to our life, so this certainly 'blows up' a common belief amongst women that we have no time to exercise!

'Regular exercise can add an average of seven years to our life.'

Christiane Northrup, M.D.,

in *Women's Bodies, Women's Wisdom*

Exercising can be as simple as running, or even walking, outdoors for a breath of fresh air, or following a free, fifteen-minute exercise program on YouTube every day. My little secret is to do either running or walking with inspirational music in my ears! I have also been practicing yoga for ten years and have found it a very subtle and effective way to keep grounded through the mind-body synchronisation. And it is also a useful reminder ... to breathe! My favourite online yoga teacher is Adriene because she is keen to show how you can be kind to your body when it is not 'cooperating', which of course does happen some days. Medical experts recommend that you need to exercise at least three days a week and for thirty minutes each time to feel and see the benefits.

'Disease is a foreign thing. It inhabits us to bother us into making necessary spiritual changes.'

Grandmother Bernadette, in C. Schaefer's
Grandmothers Counsel the World

Emotional health

Though emotions cannot actually be '*touched*', I have chosen to discuss them a little more here, besides in Chapter Two, because they form the next layer of our 'being', directly after what is visible to the eye, and they directly affect the neurology and chemical secretions in our body. What we eat, and whether we exercise, also affect our emotions, as does countless other parameters. Here, however, we will explore some self-help ways to transform negative emotions into positive ones, especially when they are produced by our untamed 'monkey mind'.

Gratitude: This is the most instant and most powerful way to feeling good that I know of. We often forget to focus on what we already have in our lives, instead of on that one, single 'thing' that we do not have! When the hairs on your arm rise with the warm feeling of gratitude, you know you are doing it right, and from the heart. The practice below works miracles for me. Try it out and watch the magic happen in your life!

> **PRACTICE #12**
>
> **Self-influence towards authenticity –
> Gratitude: 5 minutes, 5 things**
>
> Make notes on a piece of paper or in your beautiful notebook five things, moments or people's actions or words that you are truly grateful for in this day. It is best to do this just before you go to bed at night. This places you in a happy state before going to bed, diluting your stressful thoughts.
>
> Also, your first morning thought will be a positive one. When you do this for twenty-one consecutive days, it will become a new empowering habit and you will find yourself practicing grateful living. You will be back into the flow of life again.

Meditation: Even five minutes a day focusing on our breath while grounded on a cushion or chair, or even on being grateful about our life, makes a substantial difference to our mood and therefore our heart's coherence. And it is OK to cry or laugh on the cushion, as long as you stay on it for those five to ten minutes! You can refer to Chapter Two for more on this practice.

Laughter: While learning how to be a yoga laughter instructor, I discovered that, when we pretend to laugh, our body does not know the difference between a real laugh and a pretend one. The same amounts of the 'happy hormones' serotonin and dopamine are produced. So, unless you have stacks of comedy movies to watch, simply practice two minutes of pretend laughter every morning in front of the mirror in the privacy of your own bathroom. Alternatively, you could start exercising your smiling muscles more. Have you noticed how contagious it is? Or have fun training to be a stand-up comedian. I recently decided I needed to introduce more humour dinto my classes and followed an online masterclass course with the British comedian, Billy Connelly. He demonstrated that anything in life can be comical, all we need to do is be more observant and practice changing perspectives, the way you view circumstances and people. The best funny stories are, of course, our own, as long as we have the flexibility to look down at them from a 'balcony view', as if we are watching ourselves in the scene.

Self-recognition: The previously discussed confusion surrounding ego and humility, our cultural conditioning of remaining invisible and our target-driven societies make us forget to celebrate our achievements. Learn how to keep your morale high by giving credit to yourself for all you have achieved so far. From such a position, not only do you have a better view but you also feel more courage! Even though it is always better to share your success with your close friend or partner, being self-led means that you can also do this alone by self-rewarding yourself.

Artistic expression: The generation of Κάλλος (*Ka-los*, emphasis on the '*a*'; Greek for 'beauty'*)* is a high-vibration activity and extremely beneficial for women, as it ignites the flow of our creative juices. Any art does this: music, dance, drawing, photography, sculpting. There are so many to choose from. We are all artists, and we are all poets.

Release and forgive: Forgiveness needs practice, and its significance for us to feel free was highlighted earlier.

Anger and our unmet needs: we will see in the next chapter that the source of anger is *needs* that we deny having, expressing or addressing. So, watch out for your angry feelings. They are a signal that you are out of balance, and it is *your* responsibility to find a way to satisfy them, because feeling anger and frustration are not only detrimental to those around you but also affect one's mental and physical health. Notice the differences between the two tachogram diagrams below . They were taken from the same person in different emotional states. Appreciation creates a smooth, stable, sine-wave-like pattern of heart rate variability (HRV), whereas frustration produces a more incoherent, disordered pattern. And, contrary to old belief, it is not a low heart rate that indicates a positive, balanced emotional state, but a high HRV.

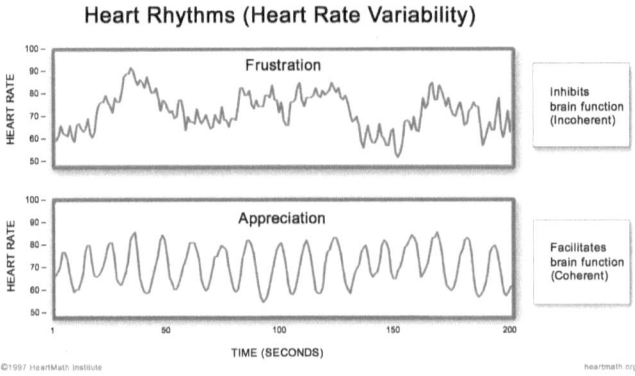

Image courtesy of the HeartMath® Institute – www.heartmath.org

Then the heart-mind-body relationship is in balance, and we have clarity of thought, high intuitive discernment and facilitate social coherence (vibes of interconnectedness and compassion towards others).

Early-morning journaling: This too was suggested as a practice earlier. See your journal as your psychotherapist. It costs you nothing and it offers you the best guidance possible, as long as you learn to trust the advice given.

I find that, by doing my practices at the same time each day, I gradually change the wiring of my brain and then it becomes a habit, just like brushing my teeth. Do not worry if initially you find it hard to allocate enough time during your day. It has been easier for me to establish healthy living patterns and maintain my interest in my body's health by mixing and matching my practices, and also by gradually freeing up more personal time, step by step. Take baby steps. Remember to be gentle and patient towards yourself, as you would for an elderly person or a child.

EXERCISE #15
Self-exploration and self-influence towards authenticity – Keep your balance

When the going gets tough, it can be very easy to lose our balance, so a brief list of ten to fifteen activities that we can do on a daily basis to keep us in balance can prove very useful. In fact, I have made a list of sixteen such activities, most of them take less than ten minutes to do. Here are some of them:

1. Go to sleep by 10pm, so that you are snoring by 10.30pm!
2. Take time out to breath fresh air in nature. Alone is fine.
3. Eat one yummy, nutritional meal with vegetables or salad every day.
4. Read one page of a book you like.
5. Laugh!!! Find reasons to laugh.
6. Sit on the meditation cushion for at least five minutes per day to catch your breath.

> So, how about making your own list? Once you complete it, you can make it more colourful and eye-catching by maybe drawing sketches on the paper or adding positive clipart images. You then can make copies of your 'Balance list' and place it in two or three areas that you regularly go into during the day as a reminder.

On a final note regarding our body's well-being, even though there are many expert authors who's books have embraced the new beliefs from this stage of our evolution, I have found one of the most informative and empowering for women to be *Women's Bodies, Women's Wisdom* by the acclaimed gynecologist, Christiane Northurp, M.D. From my own quest of healing my emotional and physical wounds, I know that self-healing is possible, and now, at the age of forty-nine, I feel stronger and more vibrant than ever before. If I can do it, so can you! All you need is to take the decision.

'Have a glance in the mirror! Your BEST friend is standing right in front of you!'

From Notes for Joy, www.artofjoy.gr

Your Wisdom: Building Trust in YOU

Many people, and predominately women, spend the largest part of their life giving their power away, because they trust those around them more than they trust themselves. Being self-led, we know what is needed at the time it is needed without feeling insecure about our ability to decide. Here, I will be suggesting some additional, alternative ways to connecting and trusting the wisdom of the inner voice, the voice of our true, authentic aelf. By trusting our voice within, we can then 'carry around with us and in us' our very own life guide as the source of our wisdom. Additionally, in this section, I would also like us to take a fresh view of the often-misused label of 'self-confidence'.

Connect with Mother Earth – Space and Silence

What comes to mind are the lyrics from Pink Martini's song, 'Splendor in the Grass'. Resting our head upon Earth's surface is indeed splendid. When I'm alone in the forest, I feel the trees talking to me and, while hugging their trunks, I feel their breathing. It is at moments like this that I remember my true nature and, in silence, hear my soul's voice. Nature's five elements are also within us: water, air (our breath), fire (our temperature), earth (our body organs, bones, muscles) and space (or 'ether', the space within us).

From time to time, I can hear Nature inviting me to slow down the pace of life and simply rest my head upon the grass and listen to it grow ...

For the moments in the day that we are not in nature, we can still connect with Mother Earth if we wish to. We can be in the middle of a job and choose to stop and relax for as little as ten seconds, with our imagination speed-travelling to an exotic beach or a glacial mountain. I always feel a peaceful, warming sensation in my core when I visualize myself resting my head upon the grass and listen to it grow, just as suggested in the lyrics of the 'Splendor in the Grass' song by Pink Martini.

By taking short, regular breaks, we keep aligning with the Earth's energies. Earth is normally quite still. So, when we too remain still, our senses line up with her stillness. This is why we would not feel an earthquake while being on a train which is moving. We need to be still in order to 'feel'.

Personally, in stillness I find I become more aware of my connection with Mother Earth. In her calmness, I also become more connected to my own biological mother, and the Universal Mother who lives and grows within me. I can then take the opportunity to be grateful that Mother Earth is always there to cradle and support me in my connection with myself, my connection with all the people, animals and plants of my micro-cosmos, and the planet as a whole. I'm grateful for the feminine energy that breathes within me, giving me the ability to love, feel joy and pain, and endure and embrace freely.

As Matt Hopwood, founder of 'A Human Love Story' project, so beautifully narrates in his book, *Mother*, he began to realise from the twenty-five stories he recorded that he, has a 'Mother' inside him. She longs to care, to give out her love and to create. Matt realised that this love stems from the presence of himself in a place which connects him to his centre, where he can honor his existence and his journey, where he can 'love his own body and hear his own voice'; and not, as he originally believed, from 'the need of being wanted by someone and needed by others, or his need of not being alone'.

So, what is 'Mother' for you? How much more 'maternal' could you become towards yourself, in order to have the resources to truly love others and lead from the heart?

Feeling our 'maternal' nature is only one of the many lessons Mother Earth gives us so generously when we learn to connect. Every part of her is a reflection of our inner world: the clouds floating in the sky are our thoughts as they pass by on the monitor of our mind. A beautiful rose with its thorns could be seen as a reflection of our inner light and darkness. The water element within us, our inner ocean, corresponds to the outer ocean of our seas. The moon cycle of twenty-eight days mirrors our menstrual cycle. By connecting, we observe, we learn.

It is important for women to be in sync with the lunar cycle. Just like the ebbing and flowing of the tides, we could take some time to notice how inward or outward we are, depending on the day in the cycle. We go inwards into the depths of our existence when we are premenstrual. We are more *yin*, contracted, dark, more fragile, more receptive of our own 'internal pain' and that of our ancestors, and more connected to our soul's calling and our truth. We know what serves and what needs to be discarded in our life. Then, as we go towards our ovulation phase, we are more *yang*, expansive, more active, out there in the world, caring, being present for others, shining our light, just like the full moon.

Up until I realised that my emotions' and body's monthly cycle was a great blessing, I would rush around like a coyote all month long. I would, in fact, get annoyed with myself that my body could not 'race' as well during menstruation. It would then of course 'talk' back at me, hoping that I would take notice, and the physical pain was awful. Again, ignoring it, I would just cover up the pain with painkillers. The worst of this situation was not my pain, however, but watching my teenage daughter curl up in agony because of *her* period pains. Like any child, she modeled her behavior and beliefs on her parent. Once I decided to change my limiting belief and saw the menstrual cycle as a blessing instead of a curse, she did too, and both of our physical pains significantly reduced. Saying this, it does not mean that women without a period are disconnected from the cycle. It is still there to support you. Let *La Luna* be your guide!

Letting go, releasing control, is so important for us women and this, indeed, is yet another lesson we can be taught by Mother Earth. We can only appreciate the cycle of life and death, and then life again, when we connect with her, the four seasons, and the complete serenity of a tree which knows with unshakable trust that, when autumn arrives, Mother Earth will not leave it naked and without leaves forever. It solidly seems to know that its leaves must die to give way for the new ones and to the buds which will give birth to fruits. It does not doubt this will happen – it lets go of worry.

Therefore, with so many gifts that she brings us, there is a responsibility and an urgency for us, as women, whose nature is creation itself, to awaken our power within and speak our truth in defense of Mother Earth, and to make caring for ecology part of all of our missions, discussions and decisions. And education of our young plays a pivotal role in this cause.

There is a multitude of ways in which we can promote the protection of our planet. Just one such ingenious and practical example landed on my desk while writing this edition of the book, through my friend Claudia Schmitz, who often mentors young women. Antonia Bartning is a young German entrepreneur, who has developed a board game for companies and organisations to understand the idea of ecology and sustainability. (You can read more about it here: www.pitchyourgreenidea.de)

Also, a concept that was initially developed by Professor Theodore Roszak and is now being developed as a separate science, is 'eco-psychology', which studies the bond of our psyche with the natural world. Eco-psychology has contributed towards finding a new, more positive message for us to be encouraged to become good environmental citizens. Advocates of eco-psychology suggest that using blame, fear and duty to get people motivated simply no longer works.

'Today, the biggest threat to humankind is not a third World War but the loss of Nature's harmony, our widening separation from Nature.'

Amma, the spark behind the 'Clean India' campaign

The Maternal Line and Our Intuition

I now want to embrace the approach of Stoic Roman Emperor Marcus Aurelius, who, in his composition of *Meditations*, which were notes he wrote to himself as a self-guide, accredited the qualities he inherited to each of his ancestors. Here is my version for my own biological parents:

'From my mother, Susan, perseverance and adaptability; the ability to reach out to people – especially when they are in need; and, also, organisational prowess and a great passion for learning.'

'From my father, Costas, remaining unruffled through tough times; persistence, courage and moderation; simplicity in the way of living, not needing much to get by, and a good work ethic.'

Regardless of who our parents or grandparents are or were, it is important to appreciate their imprints on us, and that they live inside of us whether we like it or not. As I get closer to healing my relationship with my parents, I feel that my life is taking on a whole new meaning. Understanding, release and forgiveness have been a big part of my lengthy journey. The liberating effects are far reaching and not simply contained within the family. My entire outlook on life is changing and many of my limiting beliefs are replaced with empowering ones. At last, my 'true colours' are out there for the whole world to see! I feel so FREE! They say our family is our first school of life. It is, therefore, a good idea to 'graduate' from this before we go on to get a 'university degree'. Graduation does not mean necessarily getting back together with our family if this is not possible, but it means we accept that our family is a part of us.

The elders of our planet have often been heard to say that our work in releasing the deep wounds of our past contributes to diminishing the suffering of the world as a whole. In the quantum field of possibilities, where there is no time, the healing expands in all directions: ourselves, our present family, our ancestors, our descendants, our country, our race, the world. We are in the period of 'Reversal of Consciousness', or else known as the 'Age of Meeting Ourselves Again'. So, I invite us all to re-record the story we say about ourselves and see if, while doing so, we stop blaming 'others' for our current reality.

PRACTICE #13

Self-influence towards authenticity – Releasing deep pain from our collective past or childhood

H.H. Sai Maa* suggests that we 'take our hands and place them under our abdominal area, where all our difficult emotions sit, emotions that don't allow us to go further in our lives. Let our hands be a basket for our painful emotions. Inhale into our abdomen, and exhale into our hands our lack of trust, our doubts, our sorrows. See the power. Fill our hands with light and bring all that is suffering to the Great Mother in our hearts, to the highest part of ourselves, to be healed.' [...]

'To truly love, it is necessary to drop the past and say, "I start over, right here and right now, being a new me."'

* Born in Mauritius, H. H. Sai Maa is considered a blessed Indian saint and revered spiritual teacher.

Source: Carol Schaefer, (2006), *Grandmothers Counsel the World*, Trumpeter Books, Shambhala Publications, p.141.

By honoring, connecting to, and releasing our ancestors from ancestral guilt, remorse and fear, we are given the opportunity to get an insight into the answer to the Big Question: 'Who Am I?' Our ancestors are also a great source of wisdom, which is available for us to access whenever we ask for their guidance. If you have not had such an experience already, you may well ask, 'How is this possible? They have passed away!'

'I go forth along, and stand as ten thousand.'
From Maya Angelou's Poem, 'Our Grandmothers'

Whereas extra-sensory awareness was considered an area of metaphysics and labeled as wild fantasy, scientific evidence over the past fifteen years has proven that the perceptual potential of humans is vastly underutilised. The HeartMath Institute is one of the pioneers in this field of study. Their research has shown that our heart is intuitive, and that it is not simply insightful but it also operates like a huge electromagnetic activator and receptor, which allows us to send and receive electromagnetic signals to and from the environment. Moreover, they mention another type of intuition which they have named 'non-local intuition', as it transcends time and space. The degree of sensitivity to these heightened states of awareness highly depends on the level of our heart coherence and our HRV, as mentioned earlier.

Insight is, therefore, the intuition that we build through time and experience, e.g., in a field of work, noticing body language and repetitive patterns. A taxi driver with twenty years' experience has insight when they know that the passenger they have picked up is a drug addict. Or a mother knows when her child is lying.

Energy sensitivity is our neurology's ability to tune in to the electromagnetic fields that surround us. Highly sensitive people can often be overwhelmed by the number of signals they can sense and, as a result, they can often feel emotions or physical pains that are not theirs. This does not mean that they cannot develop ways of protecting themselves from such overdoses. In fact, they can develop into excellent, compassionate leaders. The main way to tune in and remain protected is by being in the present moment, simply and mindfully connected and aware of our surroundings, no past, no future thoughts in the background of our mind. Animals have high energy sensitivity and can sense whether we are afraid of them or whether we love them and want to communicate with them.

Both energy sensitivity and insight are useful when you want to detect if somebody you meet for the first time is lying to you. Here, it is not just body language that you would sense. Osho, in his book *Intuition: Knowledge Beyond Logic*, talks about honesty and how it is connected to intuition. I have noticed that the more I use my intuition and avoid lying, the easier it becomes for me to distinguish between who is truthful and who is not. And it is only recently that one of Osho's remarks about intuition suddenly made sense. He had once said: 'When you are completely honest with someone, she or he will not be able to lie to you.' The answer was all there, staring at me on ... a morning teabag label: 'Intuition comes from innocence'! Research has shown that, on average, we lie ten times a day, sometimes without realising it ('How are you?' – 'I'm fine, thanks).

'Intuition comes from innocence.'
Osho

Osho explains further in his book that 'Intuition functions in a quantum leap. It has no methodological procedure, it simply sees things. It has eyes to see.' And, if 'its eyes' do not see, then, as Osho says, the obstacle is your unclean unconscious. He also makes a distinction between 'instinct' and 'intuition': the first needs fulfillment, whereas the second has no needs – it is freedom, independence, non-linear, feminine.

You could try out a fun exercise to test your degree of energy sensitivity in relation to your close friends and family.

EXERCISE #16
Systemic awareness and relational influence – Exercising your 'intuitive' muscles

There needs to be at least four of you, and, when one of them at random stands a metre apart from you, with you facing the wall, you can try to sense their energy pattern and identify who they are.

Obviously for this to work, the person standing behind you needs to try and be as unidentifiable as possible, i.e., silent, without any heavy, bodily movements.

Non-local intuition was scientifically discovered through tests whereby people whose brains and hearts were wired up could sense what the emotional content of a non-sequential photograph would be before it appeared on the computer screen in front of them. Such research provides evidence of the heart knowing well before the brain what will happen next. I'm sure we can all share such instances. Knowing when a car is coming around a blind bend before we see or hear it. Or sending love out to someone who lives oceans apart, and whom we have not heard from for a while, only to receive an SMS from them seconds after. We often call this 'telepathy'.

Some people are blessed to be born with the ability to intuit naturally, whereas for most of us this is dormant, but is still, nevertheless, there! We can start training ourselves to tap into our insight, or tune into these energies, even if we do not think we have this ability. Without trial and error in discerning between the soft, gentle, encouraging voice of our heart's intelligence, and the loud, hard, fearful, deterring voice of ego, we may get easily disappointed by falling into the trap of thinking that what was our intuition was, in actual fact, our wishful thinking. I would like to remind you at this point that the 'radiation' of unconditional love towards other sentient beings is what puts an end to our detachment from our environment and plugs us back into the umbilical fluid through which each and every one of us connects to others, and to the One. Often, when we think that 'it is only our imagination', it is not!

'Imagination is more important than knowledge.'

Albert Einstein

Confidence

Maybe we heard our parents or teacher say, 'She could do much better, but she lacks confidence', and then we decided to pin a label on ourselves as a reference point when we do self-talk: 'I'm not confident.' And then, that's it! We cringe at the thought of getting up in public and giving a talk, or wince when we are asked to operate the phone centre in the reception while the receptionist is on sick leave. We get badly offended when our manager suggests that we improve the way we write a report and become defensive-aggressive.

The limiting belief that we established gradually seeps into every area of our life, and then lack of confidence becomes a self-fulfilling prophecy. With it, other non-confident behavioural patterns emerge, such as aggression, defensiveness, constant apologising and excusing ourselves, or saying 'yes' to everything everybody throws at us, in order to please. But can we please everyone in this world? Where do we draw the line? When will our own needs 'take their turn' to be fulfilled? In which dark cupboard do we forget our dreams? And how do we ever get a chance to develop unconditional love and true compassion?

'The secret of successful people is that they failed one thousand times, before they succeeded only once!'

I talk from firsthand experience because the girl I described above used to be me. On my journey towards freedom, I discovered that 'confidence' is not a label someone can pin on you unless you accept it. Actually, there is another quality better suited here, as it bounces back the responsibility of our reality to us, and this is called 'self-efficacy'. Self-efficacy is our belief in our ability to succeed. This only comes through trial and error, through practicing. Ask anyone who has accomplished great things; in fact, model them! Because, if you ask them, they will surely tell you that the secret of their success is that they failed one thousand times before they succeeded only once!

So, the more practice you get, the more capable you become in an activity or skill.

Now that we have got this illusion called 'confidence' out of the way, let me see if you are up for a challenge!

EXERCISE #17
Self-exploration and self-Influence towards authenticity – What are you good at? Surely, more than you think!

Choose a quiet spot in one of your favourite places and allow some time for this, say about forty-five minutes. Make a note in your beautiful notebook of fifty things you are good at. Yes, fifty! This has been tried and tested over a period of six years on the self-leadership course I teach, so it is possible! In fact, once you go past number twenty, your pen will not be able to stop writing! These activities could be as diverse as 'I'm good at telling stories to young children' to 'I'm a champion at butterfly spotting!'

Try to complete this exercise in one go or you may never attempt it again. This list of fifty capabilities of yours serves as an excellent booster on the days you do not feel like getting out of bed, or when you are about to go to a job interview. It also shows you how multivariate and colourful you are.

You are as expansive as a rainbow that wraps itself around the whole planet. Did you know that?

Hope – Trust – Faith

The connection of faith and having faith in our own wisdom and trusting ourselves. Grace. This is an excerpt from a real-life dialogue I had while preparing for a large-scale, outdoor Christmas event:

'I tell you, it will *not* rain! Everything will be fine!! It is for a good cause! I can clearly "see" it in front of me right now! It is a starlight sky! It will be cold however! Dress well!'

'We hope so!' they respond in disbelief, continuing the conversation with a fearful voice. 'You do know, don't you, that the weather forecast is for a huge downpour of rain. Shall we at least put up a tent over the stage? What will happen to the musical instruments if they get wet? They cost a fortune!'

The first person talking here demonstrates 'faith and trust', while the second person has 'hope'.

Can you sense the subtle difference? The flavour of 'hope' has an element of 'wishful thinking', and a creeping fear that maybe this will not work out after all. It is not far from putting a wish-washy, grey colour over a brightly coloured dream. Whereas, trust in our heart's intelligence, trust in our own wisdom and deep faith in the help that will surely come our way when the motive is for the good of others, is an integral part of leadership. By this stage of this book, we very much appreciate the laws of the universe and our innate ability to *know* with our heart before our logical mind *thinks* it knows, and that we make our own reality. Faith is not rational. It is, in fact, a *leap of faith* and a courageous act of humanity because we cannot prove or touch it.

So how do we develop 'faith', the other half of creation? This is about the power of prayer. Connecting to the divine in prayer may not look at all like what we have been taught. Engaging in prayer is not necessarily a physical posture and specific words, which you observe someone doing. A farmer who is diligently ploughing his field is praying at the same time because, while doing so, he is in a state of higher consciousness and identifies with the creator. He feels the joy of collecting a rich crop in the autumn in every single cell in his body. Scientist and spiritual seeker Gregg Braden has travelled the whole planet in search of the secret of prayer. He once asked a monk who, while praying, uttered no words: 'What is it that you say inside of yourself when you pray?' The monk smiled softly and said: 'I say nothing. Prayer is a "feeling".' This may remind you of the 'visualisation technique' mentioned as a practice in Chapter Two.

A common stumbling block that often may produce phenomenally 'disappointing' results is our inability to 'let go' of how an outcome will come about, or when, in order to have our dream fulfilled, a specific other person's contribution is included. The first limits the flow of divine creativity, and the second goes against the natural law of free will of the specific person we involuntarily involve in our dream.

**'Patience, enthusiasm and optimism, these three qualities should be the mantras of our lives.
In every field, we can observe that those who have faith succeed.
Those who lack faith lose their strength.'**

Amma, from '108 Quotes on Faith'

On a personal level, an obstacle to having faith used to be the feeling that I was not worthy of asking for something to be given to me. I have now come to believe that, when we ask for something, it will move us on spiritually (and, by that, I do not necessarily mean a red sports car!), it will help us become stronger, healthier, more fulfilled and, therefore, with more energy to serve those in need around us. In this sense, asking for financial affluence gives 'money' a higher energetic vibration than the one that it is usually associated with; more 'money' to be able to serve others. In any case, the divine has no energy limitations. It can care for all beings simultaneously. And this is the stage where my own journey is right now.

The heroic lady on the front cover of this book is named 'Unshakable Hope' and is a reflection of a life philosophy of 'Trusting our own wisdom, and having faith that help WILL be provided 100% of the time.' The sun will surely rise, and it will be a Golden Dawn – not a cloud in the sky! And the Christmas event took place under a cold, clear, starlight sky, and all the young volunteers had 'Sparkles in their Eyes'. Anything is possible – you simply have to BELIEVE!

'The hand that rocks the cradle is the hand that rules the world.'

Poem title by William Ross Wallace (1819–81)

References and Further Reading

Amma, (Sri Mata Amritanandamayi Devi), (2014), *108 Quotes of Faith*, Mata Amritanandamayi Mission Trust, Kerala, India.

Moorjani, A., (2017), Interview 'On the Real Truths, Self-love, Ego and Fear' on 'Wisdom from the North' YouTube channel, https://www.youtube.com/watch?v=ih9YODzDOhI [site Accessed Dec. 2022]

Billander, S. (2009), *Meta-Health®: Consciously Healing your Body and Soul*, US.

Bradden, G. (2008), *The Spontaneous Healing of Belief*, Hay House Inc.,US.

Bradden, G. (2015), *Resilience from the Heart: The Power to Thrive in Life's Extremes*, Hay House, UK.

Chögyam Trungpa, (1984), *Shambhala: The Sacred Path of the Warrior*, Shambhala Publications, Inc., Boston, US.

Chopra, D. (2015), *Quantum Healing*, Bantam Books Publishers, NY, US.

De Saint-Exupéry, A. (1990), *The Little Prince*

Childre, D., Martin, H., Rozman, D. and McCraty, R., (2016), *Heart Intelligence: Connecting with the Intuitive Guidance of the Heart*, Waterfront Press.

Christofi, P., (2011), *Imprints*, (in Greek Αποτυπώματα), SOL Publications, Athens, Greece.

Enders, G. (2015), *The Gut*, Scribe Publications, UK.

Hayward, J. (1997), *Letters to Vanessa*, Shambhala Publications, Inc., US.

Lipton, B. (2005), *Biology of Belief*, Hay House Inc., US.

McCraty, R., and Shaffer, F., (2015), "Heart rate variability: new perspectives on physiological mechanisms, assessment of self-regulatory capacity, and health risk", *Global advances in Health and Medicine*, Vol. 4, no.1, pp.46-61.

Moritz, A. (2012), *The Amazing Liver and Gallbladder Flush*, Ener-Chi Wellness Press, US.

Moorjani, A. (2014), *Dying To Be Me: My Journey from Cancer, to Near Death, to True Healing*, Hay House Inc., US.

Northurp, C. (2010), *Women's Bodies, Women's Wisdom*, Bantam Books, Random House, Inc., US.

Nachmanovitch, S., (1991), *Free Play: Power of Improvisation in Life and the Arts*, G.P. Putnam's Sons Publishers.

Osho, (2001), *Intuition: Knowledge Beyond Logic*, St. Martin's Press, NY.

Wohlleben, P. (2018), *The Secret Network of Nature: The Delicate Balance of All Living Things*, The Bodley Head Ltd.

Shearer, A., Hunt, M., Chowdhury, M. and Nicol, L., (2016), "Effects of a brief mindfulness meditation intervention on student stress and heart rate variability", *International Journal of Stress Management*, Vol. 23, no.2, p.232.

Thubten Chodron, (2018), *The Compassionate Kitchen*, Shambhala Publications.

Yim, J., (2016), "Therapeutic benefits of laughter in mental health: a theoretical review", *The Tohoku journal of experimental medicine*, Vol. 239(3), pp.243-249.

CHAPTER 4

Your Heart, Your Voice

Now that we trust what stands true for us, our inner wisdom, we are ready to find the most effective way to express ourselves to be heard. This chapter will be demonstrating how we can use 'heart language' to do so in a powerful, assertive way, so that our voice *is* heard. We will also 'borrow' some neuro-linguistic programºmming principles regarding human rapport to see how we use our relational influence to create resonant connections with other people. Finally, we will be discussing ways of becoming better at presenting in front of a group of people.

The Power of Our Words

How do you react when someone gives you a compliment? And do you react differently if the person giving the compliment is a woman or a man? Do you accept it graciously or do you brush it away as if it was never said, or, even worse, do you dilute it by assigning the praise to somebody that helped you to be the way you are? How do we expect to be heard if the way we communicate verbally, or through our body language and energetic field, comes from a position of weakness and self-resignation? It is not being modest and unpretentious to accept a compliment and to simply say, 'Thank you' with a grateful smile! If you are still unsure about this statement, you can remind yourself of the relationship between 'humility' and 'ego', as explained in detail in the beginning of Chapter Three.

In addition to this, I wish that those of you who are finding it difficult to recondition your thinking about showing your worthiness remain gentle towards yourselves, as it takes time. Outlined below are the findings of some interesting social science research which demonstrates the difference in language used by parents while raising girls and boys. Girls, for example, are often told that they need to take care of their appearance, to be obedient and to be quiet, whereas boys are told not to cry and to be strong and decisive, and are encouraged to be sportive, even mischievous, at times. What I would like us to look at now is how we gradually become aware of its effect on us, and the way we, as women, express ourselves in order to be heard, while remaining true to ourselves.

'I will not be silent. I will be heard!'

Words of actress playing Mary Magdalene (in the progressive 2018 movie Mary Magdalene, directed by Garth Davis)

The word 'I' is a word I have struggled with for most of my life. During the first half, I was told off for using it, and through the second half, I have tried to unlearn this pattern after finding out that, when used in moderation, it allows me to authentically express what feels important to me. This of course is contrary to the common belief that, as a word, it makes us sound arrogant. During the 'Way of Council' training, our teacher taught both men and women that, when used in moderation, 'I' also allows others to feel more open and spacious in their interaction with us, because we do not oblige them to involuntarily belong to our camp of thought. So, we could say 'I believe that ...' instead of saying 'Most people believe that ...', or 'I feel that ...' instead of saying 'This makes us all feel ...', or 'I'm good at ...' instead of saying 'Women love doing ...' Can you sense the difference in vibration?

Let us now put some of these ideas to the test.

EXERCISE #18
Self-influence towards authenticity and relational influence towards resonance – Stating our ability and expressing our achievements

Make a note of your most recent achievements and then find an opportunity to share them with your partner or a friend. Make sure you try to observe yourself while doing so. What language are you using? Are you using too many words or giving away your '*shine*' to someone else? Are you mumbling? What is your body language and tone of voice? Do you feel shy or pretentious while doing so?

See if you can make this into a weekly practice: tkeep a note of your achievements, however small they may seem, and then to share them regularly with people close to you (a group of female friends is best). In this way, when the time comes to ask for promotion in work or a better salary, you will have already done a self-evaluation of your work performance, and you will also know how to express this in a succinct and powerful way, without feeling that you are a fraud!

> Remember that showing your true colours does not mean that you are not grateful for the people that helped you along the way. You can create plenty of opportunities to express your gratitude towards them.

Now, you could do the same exercise by stating your *abilities*. This will be good practice for when you design your biographical note (CV) or go for a job interview. If you do not 'show off' your abilities, who do you think will? Your parents? Fortunately, they do not allow them to be present during job interviews!

The words we use need to be very carefully chosen, as they are a direct representation of how we see ourselves. How we see ourselves is then reflected on our cosmic mirror back at us, in the eyes of the others around us. When we expose our 'authentic self' by the use of our voice, we become free from a woman's common suffering: the 'addiction of approval'. In the section about 'powerful presence', we will learn how body language and tone of voice are at least ten times more important than the actual words we utter.

EVERYTHING you do, EVERYTHING you say and the way you say it, COMMUNICATES a message to the outer world!!

> **'Your playing small does not serve the world.
> There is nothing enlightened about shrinking
> so that other people won't
> feel insecure around you.**
>
> **And as we let our own lights shine,
> we unconsciously give other people permission
> to do the same.**
>
> **As we are liberated from
> our own fear, our presence automatically
> liberates others.'**
>
> Marianne Williamson

Heart Language

Imagine this. Luciano returns from work and has the habit of throwing his clothes carelessly on the floor or on the furniture. This is a permanent source of conflict with Iris, who also works, but returns slightly earlier, in time to do some tidying up and cooking. In the following quarrel, Iris accuses Luciano of being insensitive and lazy, whereas Luciano criticises Iris for being hyper-sensitive and argues that she brings her work problems at home. I wonder what it would be like if they sat down over coffee on a Sunday morning and both expressed their needs clearly and sincerely, relating to this daily habitual pattern with the aim of finding a solution that would be mutually satisfactory.

Luciano could say, for instance: 'When I return from work, I have the need to feel free because, in the office, I feel great pressure and responsibility, so I express this by throwing all my "weights" (clothes) away.' Iris could say: 'Well, *I* feel that I'm under pressure at work too, and that, when I return home, I have the need to feel that our house is in order and clean. Although I'm also tired, I spend my time tidying up and cleaning our house. So, when *you* come home and throw your clothes around, seemingly without thinking, I feel despair that you don't respect me or appreciate my efforts, and I get very angry.'

In the previous chapter, we discussed that, in order to be truly compassionate towards others, we must, in parallel, practice self-compassion by ensuring that we also satisfy our own basic needs and desires. We learned that to identify our needs and desires means we must accept that, besides being divine, we are also human. When we are aware of our needs, then we can also skillfully find a way of satisfying them, either by doing so ourselves or by expressing them out loud and asking for the help of others. What causes us discomfort or eruption in our family and workplace relationships is when we adopt an aggressive stance in expressing them.

Anger v. aggression: expressing anger

Anger is a strong emotion which is often confused with 'aggression'. When our anger becomes externalised, it is labeled by society as 'bad behavior', or is disrespectfully linked to hormonal imbalance, especially when a woman becomes tearful or hysterical. Founder of non-violent communication (NVC), renowned world mediator and educator Dr Marshal Rosenberg used to say that 'Anger reflects an unmet need.' Anger being berated has also contributed to the commonly shared disempowering belief that personal needs are unimportant, and display egotistical, non-caring behaviour.

'It takes two to know one.'

Gregory Bateson, anthropologist, social scientist, the father of cybernetics

In her book, *Love Between Equals*, Buddhist psychologist Dr Polly Young-Eisendrath explains that 'anger' is confused with 'aggression', even amongst many of her colleagues. 'Anger', when mindfully felt or expressed, is there to remind us of, or restate, our boundaries of self-respect in relation to others. This is in contrast to 'aggression', which is violent and punitive towards others. It takes many forms, depending on our family conflict resolution role models and our own emotional balance. Aggression can, therefore, take on many forms. It may be disguised as silence and indifference, or it may take the form of bullying, rejection, scorn and verbal violence. In extreme cases, it takes the form of physical violence. Although, on saying this, psychological violence can be much more damaging in the longer term than physical violence.

As mentioned in Chapter One, Ancient Greek philosopher Aristotle prescribes the 'middle way', especially in the instances when we lash out at people who are in no way linked to the original conflict. He would teach that, 'Yes, you can be angry; however, your anger needs to be expressed in the right way, towards the person that you feel anger towards, and at the right moment.'

'Everything that irritates us about others can lead us to an understanding of ourselves.'

Carl Jung, psychoanalyst and philosopher

What often happens during heated communications, as with the example of Luciano and Iris, is that we confuse the *trigger* of our anger with its cause and get angry with the person that triggered us, whereas it is not their fault. In actual fact, it is no one's fault, because what angers us is not a person, not even our self, but the lack of satisfaction for one of our needs. Many times, we are not aware that we have this need or that it remains unsatisfied, and so, lacking its awareness, the need lingers within us and 'cries', just like a deserted child. And, as if this was not enough, we accuse the other of making us angry, so the criticism and the accusations lessen our chances of being heard even further, and of the other person feeling they might wish to fulfill our need. In this way, a vicious circle is created with no beginning or end.

The language of criticism (or language of logic and comparison) was named by the founder of NVC, Marshall Rosenberg, as the 'language of the jackal'. We were taught this language thousands of years ago and still continue to be taught it through television, social media, our family role models and, of course, through our schooling systems.

We are being raised in a highly patriarchal society, where everything is measured and compared. There are numbers and hierarchy everywhere: 'I'm the boss around here', 'You are the top pupil in class because your marks were higher than mine', 'You are younger, so you need to respect the ones older than you', 'you have studied for more years than me, so you are better educated', 'You have one thousand olive trees, so you are a real farmer compared to me who has none', 'You have a jeep, so you must be richer than me.' There are opposites everywhere: right/wrong, good/bad, beautiful/ugly, moral/immoral, love/hate.

Our schooling model, in most cases, has been to compare and criticise. This is also connected, however, to individual differences in perception of the world and in life values. So, the comparisons we make are vastly subjective. As we may have noticed, criticism creates feelings of guilt, shame and many other wounds which drain us from the joy of life, like, for example, when a parent tells off a child: 'Say you're sorry ... I can't see that you're really sorry! Say it!!'

Expressing our needs non-violently

On the exact opposite side of this setup, there is the 'language of the giraffe', the 'heart language' which uses the voice of our real, deeper needs, creating corresponding emotions. The key is to be conscious of what we need, and to express it clearly; likewise, to be able to identify, and put a name to, what it is we are feeling at any given moment. In a sense, to speak 'giraffe language' we need to continually be in a mindful state and very honest with ourselves and others. In 'heart language' there is only room for our own truth.

So, how could Iris ask for Luciano's help to fulfill her need in a non-aggressive way?

'Luciano, I feel despair and anger when I watch you throw your clothes all over the place when you come in from work, because my need for feeling respected for my contribution in keeping our home clean and tidy is not met. Would you be prepared to help me find a way to meet this need of mine to feel more respected for what I do?'

It is important to note the open, non-aggressive way that Iris uses to ask for help from Luciano. There is no expectation that Luciano will be satisfying her 'need for respect'. This attitude prepares Iris before approaching Luciano to attempt to find strategies that may satisfy her need *without* involving Luciano's contribution. Moreover, it does not make Luciano feel in any way obliged to meet her need and makes it more likely that he will sincerely want to help her in any way he can.

What alternative strategies could you think of if you were to whisper some ideas in Iris's ear? It may be obvious that the key to non-violent expression is to have no expectations from others. And, of course, in order to have no expectations from others, we need to have almost mastered the act of self-care and self-compassion. In other words, we need to know how to look after our own needs. If, however, it is impossible to do so within the environment we have chosen to be in or the people we have chosen to live with, and the need is of primary importance to us, then we may have to decide to leave the environment or the relationship in order to be kind to ourselves.

> **'Expectations are a source of suffering and take us away from giving out true, authentic, unconditional love.'**

Here is an exercise that will test your creative ability to pull yourself out of a challenging situation and observe it objectively, as well as your ability to adapt.

EXERCISE #19

Self-influence towards authenticity and relational influence towards resonance – Expressing your needs using 'heart language'

Choose a recent dialogue, either from your personal or work life, that did not go very well, or maybe ended up in an argument.

Doing this exercise for the first time, I would suggest that you do not choose a dialogue with a person that you have an ongoing conflict with, or that involves heavy forms of violence.

Practice some mindful meditation for five minutes. Then, take some time to reflect on what happened. 'Float' above the event as an independent observer and try to perceive what each of the people involved felt or may have been thinking at the time, or, more specifically, which need of theirs they wanted you to satisfy for them at the time.

The more you 'become them' and 'place yourself in their shoes', the more effective this exercise will be.

Next, place yourself in your own shoes and contemplate which of *your* needs was not met at the time. You may find it amongst the following, as humans more or less have similar basic needs:

Need to feel accepted as we are and respected for what we are	Need to feel secure
Need to be free to choose what we want and what we say	Need to be deeply listened to
Need to be free to take care of our physical requirements (e.g., sleep)	Need for feeling and being creative
Need for intimacy	Need for fun and laughter

Once you have identified the unfulfilled needs, especially your own, write down:

- A list of strategies (ways) that your need could be fulfilled without the involvement of the person or people that you had the argument with. Take your time to be as creative as you can. See if you can come up with three alternatives!
- A short monologue of what you would say in the same situation, if you could replay the whole scene again. Use the example of the structure of Iris's wording above.

Having completed the exercise, how do you feel about the argument now? Do you feel ready to make this exercise into a practice when engaging in challenging situations?

'The challenge for us is not to avoid conflict or "win the argument", but to resolve it in a dignified, compassionate way for all involved, including ourselves.'

It is unrealistic to expect that we can go through life without conflict arising at some point. The spiritual challenge for us is not to avoid it or 'win the argument', but to resolve it in a dignified, compassionate way for all involved, including ourselves. Using 'heart language', as you may appreciate by now, requires constant mindfulness, self-exploration, a fair amount of awareness of others around us, and, of course, the willpower to resonate. Unlearning our habitual patterns takes effort, patience and gentleness towards ourselves, and involves being courageous to take every possible opportunity to practice – to practice a lot! Above all, while trying to engage in 'heart language' we need to remain centred in our heart area, so that we not only talk from the heart but we first and foremost *listen* from the heart.

The Art of Active Listening

Listening from the heart is indeed an art. Some people are born with an innate talent in this. Often, the real artists in this are our grandparents: people who have no need to hurry to go anywhere, people who simply 'ARE', people who have experienced life to its fullest. Can you remember a time when you were listened to attentively? For me, it was as if

I were transported to an altogether different realm, and I became the centre of the universe. For those of us who have been brought up in a family or a society of speed and high, masculine energy, active listening as part of 'dialogue' has not been shown to us. We may subconsciously copy our first role models and only use our ears and thinking function to listen, instead of the 'ears of the heart'. Often, therefore, while the other person is talking, we may catch ourselves parallel-talking inside our head: maybe judging, maybe comparing, maybe feeling argumentative and maybe preparing what we will be saying next; maybe even, trying to see how we can manoeuvre the conversation towards our pre-fixed agenda, to achieve the expected outcome we desire.

The 'Way of Council' practice mentioned earlier mirrors the feminine way of communicating. When you sit in the Circle, you may have a topic in mind, however it may never be discussed, since the space created auspiciously 'listens' to the on-the-spot needs of the collective consciousness of the Circle. The discussion is organic and mirrors 'whatever arises', with no agenda in mind. It resembles the meandering of a quiet river. Sometimes, the most powerful listening experiences have come when a Circle member 'talks' in silence.

On a personal level, I find sitting in a Circle extremely therapeutic and liberating compared to the dense and heavy vibration of board meetings and their fixed, linear agenda. And you can rest assured that, in a Circle, whatever needs to be solved does get solved.

'Active listening' is, in a sense, 'compassionate listening'. In relation to being compassionate with others, the story of the nun in Chapter Three reminds us that to listen actively and mindfully means that momentarily we are merged with the person sitting opposite us, so that we get into their shoes. Then we can understand with our mind, and feel with our heart, what they are thinking and what they are feeling. I will also, nevertheless, add an extra element into this composition which is related to self-compassion: if we are new to self-empowerment, simply making listening a one-way action may place us in a position of weakness and throw us totally out of balance.

On my own journey to self-empowerment, there have been many occasions when a family member or a colleague was talking to me on the phone (or face to face) and I would get completely drawn into the meaning of the words they were using. So, while I was listening to them, I would be very 'up in my head' instead of in my heart. I would, therefore, ignore their tone of voice (or body language) and, more importantly, forget to feel what the energy they vibrated felt like on my body. By the end of their monologue, and even days later, I would realise that they had spoken to me in a subtle, yet aggressive way (using sarcasm, derogatory comparison, mockery, etc.). When we feel more in our 'seat of power' and are in a continuously mindful state, we can curtail such monologues, or, if for some reason we choose to listen to them, they leave us untouched.

Resonance

While entering a room, we have already communicated before we even open our mouth to talk. This is because, as we have mentioned before, our body radiates electromagnetic energy and we unconsciously pick up on the vibrations. The heart-brain connection is activated, and then emotions, thoughts, memories and beliefs are stirred up. In the 1970s, Professor Albert Mehrabian of the University of California in Los Angeles performed a series of studies on human communication, and he discovered that, in the majority of cases, what resonates with another person when someone is 'sending' a message (stimuli) is not the words they chose to use (7 percent) or their meaning, but their non-verbal communication: tone of voice (38 percent) and body language (55 percent). For example, when words and body language disagree, we tend to believe the body language. We will explore how we can enhance our non-verbal communication in the next sections of this chapter.

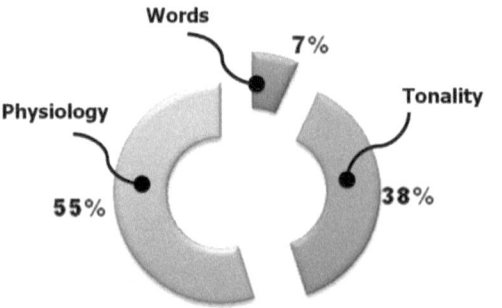

The importance of non-verbal communication

The following are some of the *key premises for creating resonance* in our communications. They mostly come from the field of neuro-linguistic programming.

1. *Have the intention of resonating with every person you interact with.* Keeping this intention in mind will not only help you allow for a spacious and open communication to take place but will also transmit positive energy vibes to the other person.

2. *Be 100 percent in the PRESENT.* Thinking that 'He normally lies so he will certainly lie to me again' is us living in the past; or thinking that 'If I say this, she will think I'm pompous' is us living in the future. My best lectures have been when I have entered the classroom unprepared yet totally present.

3. *Establish rapport.* Mirroring or matching the other person's physiology and tonality, even behaviour, occurs naturally when we are focused in the NOW. In such a state, it is as if we have both tuned into the same channel. An example of this would be a couple who are deeply in love, or some children who pick up on the tonality of their best buddy in school and sound exactly like them when they come home.

4. *Respect other people's model of the world.* In Chapter Two, we saw how we each perceive a different 'reality' based on our own values and beliefs.

5. *Stop 'mind-reading'.* Thinking that we have telepathy with the person we communicate with is a trap that often leads to invalid assumptions.

6. *'The meaning of the communication is the response you get.'* The responsibility for the other person understanding the meaning of our message the way we intended it lies largely with us. Mindfully observing the reaction of the listener to our delivered message gives us the opportunity to ask them for feedback and to clarify our communication further.

7. *'The map is not the territory.'* The words we use are not the factual representation of the event or the item they represent. Just like when we say our name, the 'name' does not mean that *that* is all of who we are.

8. *Every behaviour is motivated by a positive intent.* As difficult as it may be to believe this at times, we are all seeking to love and be loved. We are all seeking to connect.

9. *There is no such thing as 'failure', only feedback!*

10. *Practice makes perfect.*

EXERCISE #20
Self-influence towards authenticity and relational influence towards resonance – Rapport vs dissonance

Try this exercise with a friend, or better still with someone that you do not know very well (maybe a colleague or a fellow student). Sit face to face at a distance of about 1 metre apart and start talking to your pair about a subject that you are normally enthusiastic about – for example, a hobby. While doing so, try to make your body language communicate exactly the opposite of enthusiasm – i.e., boredom, anger, sadness.

Place your body in such a way that you sit cross-legged and turned away from facing your pair.

Next, ask your pair to repeat a similar interaction.

- Discuss between you how it felt.
- Were you comfortable doing it?
- Was the lack of rapport obvious?
- How did the receiver of the communication message feel?

> **'When you trip and manage not to fall, you are then a BIG STEP forward!'**
> Greek proverb

Powerful Presence

Presence is a perception. In other words, our level of presence is determined by those around us and not by how big an impact we believe we have. According to research carried out by the 'Task Force for Talent Innovation' in Manhattan, US, in 2014, on 'Executive Presence', the mainly male, senior executives of eighty-two multinationals, when asked what 'The most important quality for leadership is', responded that it is 'gravitas' (66 percent), next was 'communication' (28 percent) and next was 'appearance' (5 percent). For Asian-based multinationals, the order was still the same, but 'communication' scored a little higher at 35 percent and 'gravitas' a little lower. By 'gravitas' they meant impact, credibility, poise, decisiveness, emotional intelligence, remaining composed under pressure, charisma and vision. 'Communication' was about how concise one is and how compelling one sounds; degrees of assertiveness, humour and an ability to 'read' the environment. Finally, 'appearance' was scored on the degree of their dress being well groomed and sophisticated, on how fit and vivacious they looked and on their degree of physical fitness. On the bottom line, the research showed that 'executive presence' is not about performance but is about the subconscious signal we put out. This, of course, is a heavily skewed, masculine perception as to what counts in a leader, and less in keeping with the urgent need for a more compassionate, ecologically sound approach to leadership. Nevertheless, it serves in raising our awareness of what the situation is at present, and where we could be heading if we wanted to create a better future.

The findings from the '2017 Global Information Security Workforce Study', carried out by Frost and Sullivan, were prophetic. The fast-growing cybersecurity industry 2022 forecasts for a global 1.8 million worker shortage were exceeded. Top skills required by the industry's hiring managers still are communication and analytical skills. In my view, the communication skills requirement reflects the need for a more feminine approach to the way technology is used. It also represents an opportunity for women from non-IT/engineering backgrounds to enter the industry, since most hires have in the past been from a non-technical background, with 33 percent of the people hired rising to senior managerial levels. The study illustrates an optimistic insight on a shift in the perceived value of feminine traits being present in an otherwise male workplace environment.

Overall, in companies and organisations where servant, compassionate leadership styles are established, a 'powerful presence' would be determined by virtues such as the *yin*-related elements of warm-heartedness, humility and grace, and the more *yang*-related trio of command-integrity-clarity.

Aspects of powerful presence

Warm-heartedness and loving-kindness evolve from the compassionate nature of a leader, as already covered extensively in this book. Humility has also been discussed previously. Nevertheless, as a reminder, what is meant here is the willingness to listen tentatively, to be honest as to not knowing all there is to know, to be willing to seek advice and evaluation, to nurture leadership qualities in all members of our team in preparation for the 'next generation', and to always have the mentality of a 'beginner'.

To me, the word 'grace' brings to mind an elegant ballet dancer, or the stride of a gazelle. Within a company or organisation, 'grace' not only shows in the appearance or manner we 'hold' ourselves but also in the way we mediate through challenging situations. 'Grace' also requires a high degree of emotional intelligence and precision.

I have recently come to realise that a powerful, supportive force for humility and grace is humour. The word has its routes in the Indo-European word 'ghôm', in English 'humus', the compost pile used to naturally fertilise new growth, in Greek, 'χυμός' (himos, emphasis on the 'o'), meaning juice, the juice of life. Stephen W. Gilbert, in his work 'Etymologies of Humor: Reflections on the Humus Pile', beautifully links humour with the humble life-giving humus pile, humility and humanity. And to this effect explains that:

'... the relation between humus and humanity touches on what is best about us. Our ability to give without expectation of reward, but with the confidence that our giving is a valued contribution. The knowledge of the rightness of unconcerned giving, complete willingness to contribute to the ongoingness of life, seems combined as well, with the knowledge that a certain style of material perfection is possible. The knowledge that we end as matter that continues to be used, that is, in fact, recycled purposefully, can be cause for great comfort. And for great laughter.'

Making fun of myself being a manager for the first time is one of the anecdotal stories I share with my students. It always makes them laugh, connecting me to them and them to the elusive art of managing other people, where managing ourselves is hard enough to do in the first place. In his BBC Maestro class on 'How to become a stand-up comedian', the renowned British comedian Billy Connelly demonstrates that anything in life can be comical, and all we need to do is be more observant and practice changing perspectives. A skill not only supportive of humility and grace but also of commanding ourselves during unpredictable, challenging situations.

'Command' is related to our ability to remain composed and decisive in a non-aggressive way. It comes from the natural, inner energy we exhume when we are authentic, when we *are* our true self. It is received by others like the sun to the Earth, aligned and nurturing. 'Integrity' is also a natural extract of authenticity. You cannot be authentic and lack sincerity and stability. Finally, 'clarity' is related to wisdom, discernment and precision, which follow on from a high degree of connectivity to our insight and self-trust.

In the chapter on 'How to Invoke Magic' in his book *The Sacred Path of the Warrior*, Chögyam Trungpa Rinpoche talks about invoking 'external and internal *drala*' energies, which only descend into our existence on carefully prepared 'fertile soil', and when we are brave enough to free ourselves from self-deception. 'External *drala*' refers to the magic which we invite into our environment, by taking care of all the details, keeping it clean, uncluttered and beautiful. 'Internal *drala*', which in my mind corresponds to 'presence', is how we pick up our glass to drink water and how well our clothes fit us. When we decide to use our voice or be silent is also a mark of 'presence'.

Invoking both 'external and internal *drala*' produces 'secret *drala*'; our environment is sacred, and so are we, by way of the flawless synchronisation of our body and mind. And here comes the best part! 'Secret *drala*' gives us the magical experience of raising what the Tibetan culture calls the 'wind-horse' (*lungta* in Tibetan).

'Presence is a state of inner spaciousness.'

Eckhart Tolle in *Oneness with All Life*

This experience can be described as riding a powerful horse in a very strong wind. So, no matter what the circumstances in our lives, we are not swayed or unbalanced. We remain in the saddle, and we simultaneously draw upon the strength of the full force of the wind. In other words, the energy which we radiate when riding the 'wind-horse' is, in effect, the invocation of our sacred, powerful presence.

EXERCISE #21

Relational influence towards resonance – Introduce yourself in less than a minute and make an everlasting first impression!

This is an opportunity for you to practice presenting yourself in a professional setting; for instance, during the lunch break at a conference. Remember that it is down to us to make an everlasting impression. Also remember that in such an environment, it is essential for people to remember our name.

So, there are two succinct messages you will want to convey to the person you are introducing yourself to: a/ your name and surname, and b/ what it is you do. For both of these messages, tonality of voice and body language (handshake, genuineness of smile and eye contact) are

> important. For the second message in particular, you may want to try and encourage the other person to be intrigued by you and ask you more.
>
> What is it that you could tell them that you do that would evoke a second question and a dialogue? (Tip: You could start by saying, 'I help ... to ....')

Presenting in an Empowered Way

Picture a twenty-one-year-old junior executive who is having a panic attack at the airport. She has just missed her flight to a faraway city to present the annual marketing plan to the company's 200 salesmen. She must somehow get there, so she has no choice but to catch the next available flight out. This is her first ever presentation. She stays up all night making notes of what she will say and practices her talk, in her pyjamas, in front of the hotel room mirror.

Sleepless, the next morning she enters the huge conference room and is taken aback by what 200 people look like when they are all gathered together. She is shown to the front, and reluctantly sits along with the other presenters – her fellow colleagues, who are her seniors. While waiting her turn, she cannot help but admire the air of confidence transmitted by the presenters before her. By the time her turn comes, she is trying desperately to catch her breath and her legs are like jelly. The lights are on, and the audience has ... disappeared!

This was my first experience of presenting and, as you can imagine, it was somewhat traumatic. Since then, I promised myself two things: a/ I would never miss a flight again, and b/ I would drastically improve my presentation skills.

Professor of biology and neurological sciences Robert Sapolsky says that presentation phobia increases our adrenaline levels as high as that of a gazelle trying to escape a leopard. The differences are that we will most probably live to see another day after we have presented, as opposed to the unfortunate gazelle. And that we, as humans, are not capable of easily lowering our adrenaline once the 'danger' ceases to exist, whereas if the gazelle manages to escape, she can be found happily grazing on nearby grassland five minutes after the attempt on her life. On such occasions, adrenaline (which is normally a 'good' hormone because it 'kicks us' into action) remains in our blood stream for far too long, producing highly toxic waste. If we become stressed regularly, toxic waste accumulates over time and results in dis-ease. This is the 'fear-ful' way of getting you to improve on your presentation skills, assuming that they need improvement, of course.

The positive, alluring way would be if I told you that, by delivering an unforgettable presentation, you will have crossed the 'red line' of your limits and will have started a habit of breaking them. If you are reading this book, I'm sure you already know the feeling of breaking your upper limits at least once. It can only be described as 'riding the wind-horse'!

There is, of course, a well-kept secret with presenting: 'Practice makes perfect.' It is an art with a variety of techniques and styles, so anyone can become an effective presenter. However, in order to become a 'powerful' presenter, or better yet an 'enchanting' presenter, you still need one more little secret: where to find the bravery to overcome the fear of judgment. If I have done a good job of writing this book, you should know the answer by now.

Yes, of course you know ... you have to go within!

The dive into our inner ocean of existence first happens with the breath. The destination is our heart centre. So, we need to take a few moments for contemplation and connection with our true self.

Every time we do a presentation or make a speech, we do so in order to create a shift in the perception of our audience. In other words, it is to de-solidify fixed beliefs or, at least, to make them 'feel a little uneasy about their existence'. It could also be in order to speak *in support* of another person, in a meeting or as a witness at a court case, or *about* another person at a wedding or a funeral. In my view, taking the 'stage' requires all of the qualities of 'powerful presence', and is *always* for a noble cause.

Over and above that, it can be fun, and it challenges your intelligence as well. In preparation for such an event (when there is time to prepare), I will share with you the teachings I have collected from my own experience and training.

1. *Dive deep inside yourself*, using your breath, maybe through meditation, and connect with your heart centre. Ignite your heart intelligence.

2. Practice increasing your ability to *look at your audience through your peripheral vision* instead of your foveal vision. The first ignites your subconscious mind, lowers your stress levels and helps you enter 'the zone' or be in a state of 'flow'. In this state, you no longer need to memorise and use your logic to communicate your message. You connect to a higher realm and, in essence, you become a channel for a higher order message. When the tennis ball comes rushing towards Iga Swiatek, a top tennis player, she certainly does not go through the whole list of tennis strokes before she strikes the ball. She intuitively hits it back from a state of 'flow'.

3. Define and *keep the intention* at the centre of your mind. Why are you doing this? What is the higher purpose? There is always one!

4. Remember the 7-38-55 percent communication rule. It is more about the delivery than the content. So, plan your preparation time accordingly, and *practice, practice, practice* until you get your tonality and body language right. Also, practice radiating sun energy (see below the notes on presentation delivery). This does not mean that you will not fly 'freestyle' on the day and be authentically YOU. Practice does have a positive impact on the outcome, especially when you have little experience of presenting.

5. *Get inspired* by good speakers. There are plenty of them online. My favorite are TED Talks, as they are short, to the point and avoid 'death by PowerPoint'.

6. Engage in *positive self-talk* frequently and use the *visualisation* technique we have discussed in Chapter Two. Do not forget to feel the feelings of enthusiasm, happiness and powerful presence *as if* you are doing the presentation in the present moment.

7. *Prepare a story*. Any idea or new belief can be transformed into a 'journey'. This can serve as a metaphor. For instance, nature serves as a great source of metaphors. Life and death, beginnings and endings, spring and winter. Prepare it in such a way that the end of your story is unveiled only at the very end of your presentation. This keeps your audience in suspense. In fact, you can use the three-summit paradigm: Act 1 presents the hero's problem, Act 2 is about the hero's journey

and the challenges they face on the route to freedom, Act 3 the solution and the hero's transformation.

8. If you can, introduce an element of humour. You can use a personal short story of you making a mess of a situation. This will form a wonderful bridge of common humanity with your audience. They will also think that if you are a normal human being making mistakes, then they too can get where you are.

9. Choose a maximum of *three basic messages* you want to convey. People cannot retain more, even if you are talking for half an hour.

10. Introduce 'intervals' and an opportunity for interaction. The average attention span is less than ten minutes. It is important that you adopt a dialogue and not a lecture style for engaging with your audience. The most effective way to do this is by taking them for a journey by using guiding, rhetoric questions, such as: 'So, what do I mean by "entropy"? ... By "entropy", I mean the lack of order.'

11. *Keep it* as *'lean'* as possible. You can do away with technology or keep slides to a minimum, be light-handed on the words and use cleverly chosen images to convey the message. 'A picture is worth a thousand words.'

You can structure the content of your presentation around the '4-MAT presentation model', which borrows principles from neuro-linguistic programming, about people's different preferred ways of internalising information. It was devised by Bernice McCarthy and David Kolb.

Why? This needs to come first to satisfy people who need to hear why it is worth listening to you. What is the value of what you have to say?

What? Here you will place your concepts and supporting facts/evidence, preferably in numerical form.

How? How is this teaching/idea applicable? More for the kinesthetic types in your audience, get them to *do* something, to interact with the person next to them or with you.

What if? This is the opportunity for Q&As and testing the idea or variations of the idea. This last part is also an opportunity for you to receive feedback and expand your idea even further.

There is plenty of time to apply the '4-MAT model' even when your presentation is for five minutes.

And here are some avenues for feeling and being empowered while delivering your presentation:

1. Take almost a minute before opening your mouth to enter into a state of presence.

2. Stabilise your out-breath and in-breath, and readjust your body so that you avoid slumbering into the 'banana' posture. Keep your feet one fist-width apart, for more stability. Your body needs to be centred.

3. Establish eye contact with your audience.

4. Smile generously from the heart with a thought of gratitude for them taking time out to hear your talk and with a feeling of fulfillment for the gift that you are about to give them. Remember your intention.

5. Imagine that your whole body is the sun, radiating its beams right to the far end of the room, outside the room, outside the outskirts of the town, the country, the planet. Keep remembering you are talking to human beings, just like yourself. They have emotions too, so expand and connect with their hearts through the raising of the vibrations of your own radiating energy.

6. Keep focused on your in-breath to remain connected with your heart and your powerful, authentic self at all times. The out-breath will take care of itself.

7. Use your in-breath as an opportunity to introduce intervals, as all good musicians do. Silence can be very powerful and thought-provoking.

8. Lower the pitch of your voice.

9. Slow down your pace if you normally rush through presentations.

10. And, of course, remember to enjoy doing it! It is FUN! After all, it is YOUR VOICE they are listening to!

'Air matters, because we breathe our thoughts! All speech is out-breath, all in-breath is thought.'

Caroline Goyder, voice coach and author of Gravitas

References and Further Reading

Chögyam Trungpa, (1984), *Shambhala: The Sacred Path of the Warrior*, Shambhala Publications, Inc., Boston, US.

Bateson, G. (2000), *Steps to an Ecology of Mind*, The University Press Chicago Press, US.

Caroll, M. (2007), *Mindful Leader*, Trumpeter Books, US.

De Saint-Exupéry, A. (1990), *The Little Prince*

Gilbert, W. S. (1996), Etymologies of Humor: Reflections on the Humus Pile, *Sincronía*, Winter.

Goyder, C., (2014), *Gravitas: Communicate with Confidence, Influence and Authority*, Vermilion Publishing Co, UK.

Marshal, R. (2015), *Nonviolent Communication: A Language of Life*, 3rd Edition, PuddleDancer Press, US.

Marshal, R. (2005), *The Surprising Purpose of Anger: Beyond Anger Management: Finding the Gift*, PuddleDancer Press, US.

Northurp, C. (2010), *Women's Bodies, Women's Wisdom*, Bantam Books, Random House, Inc., US.

Reynolds, G. (2011), *The Naked Presenter: Delivering Powerful Presentations with or without Slides*, New Riders, Pearson education, CA, US.

Tolle, E.(2008), *Oneness With All Life*, Penguin Group Publishers, US.

Zinmerman, J. and Coyle, V., (2009), *The Way of Council*, 2nd ed., Bramble Books, US.

Young-Eisendrath, P. (2019), *Love between Equals: Relationship as a Spiritual Path*, Shambhala Publications Inc., Colorado, US.

CHAPTER 5

Lead By Example

We are all sitting around the table to discuss the book, but Anne,** the chairperson, has other plans. She has prepared a surprise for us. The waiter serves us all with bowls with one scoop of vanilla ice cream each. She instructs us to close our eyes and imagine that we have never tasted ice cream before in our entire life. Then she says: 'While keeping your eyes closed, take half a spoonful and allow the ice cream to partially dissolve in your mouth, and, taking your time, see whether you can follow each sensation as the first spoonful of ice cream travels towards your stomach. Remember this is your first time ever!'

The tide is going out on an enormous sandy beach. As a man strolls along the beach, he notices from a distance the silhouette of a young woman close to the water's edge. She bends forward, then makes an arching movement with her arm, takes two small steps and then bends down again, draws another arch, two more steps and then another arch. He thinks to himself, 'How odd! She must be engaged

---

** This is a true story, and I chose it to be part of this book as a tribute to Anne Lybaert, who knew how to enjoy life to its fullest. The 'starfish story' was originally authored by Loren Eisley, and as for the last story, it is no longer easy to track down who the original author is. I nevertheless thank them for their wisdom.

in a dance ritual.' While walking towards her, he notices that the beach is covered with starfish. Each time she bends down, she picks up a starfish and throws it back into the water. By now, the man is very curious. He asks her, 'What are you doing?' She replies in surprise, 'Throwing the stranded starfish back into the ocean.' He thinks, 'This is futile and silly!' and remarks out loud, 'Don't you realise that there are miles and miles of beach, and there must be thousands of starfish out here?' Smiling, she bends down again, gently picks up one more starfish, and, as she is throwing it back into the sea, she serenely replies, 'It certainly makes a difference to this one!'

Two salespeople are sent by the same company to sell shoes to an area where people walk around barefoot. After their first day, they each report back to their manager. One sends a message that says, 'These people wear no shoes; they are obviously too poor to buy any! Please send me to another area. I'm on my way back.' The other, however, sends a different message: 'Send me as much stock as you possibly can! These people are wearing no shoes. I'm sure I can sell them at least two pairs each! What an opportunity!! Thank you so much for choosing to send me here!'

For me, these three stories outline the archetype of a fully empowered compassionate leader:

- Experiencing every moment as if it is our first time: awake, vivacious, deeply connected to life, with the innocence of a child – creative living at its fullest.

- Passionately caring for all sentient beings by trusting our own wisdom, upholding unshakable faith and leading by example, no matter how small or futile the action may seem.

- Engaging with others with intelligent optimism by clearly seeing behind the mirror of our mind's limitations.

Our era signifies 'The Golden Dawn of Compassionate Leadership'. There is a plenitude of signs and movements across the planet with women rising and men supporting their climb. The ground is fertile, so I simply know that once we women develop the courage to use our voice to speak our truth and then live it by leading by example, we *already* have all the resources we need, and our 'backs *will* be covered' by forces seen and unseen. The force *is* with us!

This is much like the seven riches of a ruler found in the ancient texts of India. Here, I offer an adapted version of my own interpretation, having come across this idea in Chögyam Trungpa Rinpoche's book, *Sacred Path of the Warrior*.

The first richness of a ruler is attained by you having a close friendship with yourself, and, if possible, by living with a partner who reflects your light and darkness and bears witness to your life, and who encourages you to maintain your decency.

The second richness is having a 'counselor': a friend who unconditionally loves you and can provide you with advice from a different angle to help you see the other side, when your vision gets clouded.

The third richness of a ruler is the 'general': another fellow-warrior friend who fearlessly protects you, and is by your side when needed, in an actionable way.

The fourth richness is a 'horse'. This represents your 'wind-horse' energy which rises over and above all of life's challenges without backing down unnecessarily.

The 'elephant' is the fifth richness of a ruler. This is connected with the ruler's quality of command. The ruler moves forward at a steady pace, without being swayed or sidetracked.

The sixth richness is the 'wish-granting jewel', the open, nonchalant quality of a ruler who generously shares any 'wealth' attained.

Finally, the seventh richness of a ruler is the 'wheel', which signifies taking full responsibility for the direction of their life: heart-mind-body working in complete coherence with each other. There is a deep understanding of the universal truths, and that all is part of One and, therefore, intimately interconnected.

Learning How to Die While You Are Still Alive

As I prepare for my second reinvention of who I am, I'm excited to be returning soon to Crete and to enter the new chapter of my life. My intention is to live a more fluid, meaningful existence where I consciously create my own reality. I feel as if I have made it, and this, I know now, takes practice. As Wayne Dyer would have said: I have learned how to die while I'm still alive. Three years ago, I shook the material foundations of my twenty-two years of living in Greece: I sold my comfortable, sunny home, resigned from my 'prestigious' and safe job at the University in Crete, and set off on an adventure into 'white space', the Great Unknown. Now I find myself once again in the driver's seat. I have resigned from my job here in the UK and Libby (my car) will be driving me back across wintery Europe to Crete.

By way of explaining the 'learning how to die while still being alive' attitude, I will share with you a quick scene that took place after my first traverse across Europe During covid. A worldly businessman asked me, 'So which was your favourite city?' No hesitation there, and I know I disappointed him. I had been to no famous cities. I chose to adopt a 'going with the wind' attitude by embracing the unfamiliar. No planning ahead the routes and border crossings, no pre-booking night stays. My old self had been indoctrinated all these previous years by the American MBA style strategic thinking mindset, where having a goal and a well thought-out plan were key. Not only had I been trained to think like that, but I also came from a family were organising and planning were a way of life. Thinking out all possible future scenarios was the solution to 'controlling' circumstances and mitigating all unforeseen dangers. My DNA make-up to control outcomes and remain safe was reinforced by my teaching strategic management for fifteen years. Knowing your 'hows' and 'wheres' were apparently crucial for a secure and successful landing.

To pacify good, old Alexia, who was totally thrown into uncharted waters and often felt anxious, I (the soon-to-be-new Alexia) gave her a 'goal' to hold onto for when waters would be rough. 'We' had a British passport, so 'we' could head for the UK and the bright city of Brighton, which was familiar and friendly. This also satisfied my Greek friends and family who were shell-shocked by my decision. Even though I was fifty-one at the time, they must have secretly thought this was a midlife crisis and a result of the severe bullying I had suffered for years in work by my male colleagues for daring to adopt an 'alternative' style of teaching. For a while, I too sometimes thought that I had been driven away by my circumstances. Although I had stood up and courageously told my truth in one final committee meeting, which included the university's vice chancellor, freedom of speech ignited my metamorphosis but was not the source of my willpower.

At the time, I could hear my psyche constantly hogging me with this question: 'How would you feel if on your dying breath you looked back on your life and saw that you chose to remain in the comfort zone of your little island instead of venturing into new experiences and exploring new sides of yourself?' Freeing my spirit to my highest potential and not regretting 'not doing it' were my driving forces.

Without realising it, as I mentioned in the Introduction of this book, the road trip became a trip inside the darkest and surprisingly, also, the brightest corners of my existence, creating a continuous roller coaster of emotions. Looking back on my journey of a year out, my low moments – those of loneliness and fear– were the efforts of the dying, old self to hang onto the familiar and go into hibernation. Then these moments often produced symptoms of death and hours, even days, of mourning. Entangled in these moments were others of great joy and excitement, as I had yet again trusted that all will be well and that the world *is* after all a friendly place. Immersing myself in nature and her dance was the strategy I used to ensure that I kept a perspective of how precious my life is. There, standing by the trees or spotting a fox, I would feel gratitude for having been guided by challenging events and people to press the 'reset' button of my existence!

Much like a horse's blinders, my old rigid planning pattern of behaviour would have caused me to miss out on these opportunities and limit my horizon of expansion and growth. My openness to the unexpected and my willingness to not plan as usual blessed me with moments of supreme bliss and connection with bright, enchanting people and nature's magnificence.

This is pretty much like the old saying, 'You can only get new outcomes if you change the method you used to produce them.' Change your thoughts, change your emotions, change your behaviour, change your personality. That is when you change your personal reality.

I nearly turned around to come back to Greece three days into the journey, because my greatest fear had materialised: my fear of getting lost. My mobile phone that gave me direction through Google Maps had blacked-out just outside Lago di Garda in Italy, and I had to find my way to a neighbouring city without a navigation app. This is how I discovered that I *do* after all have a sense of direction. An *internal* navigation system!

In Belgium, I connected with vivacious Robin, an American lady larger than life who kept visiting the area of Waregem to commemorate her great great uncle and the men who lost their lives in World War One.

She is an active member of 'Brothers in Arms', a global organisation with a mission to pay respect to all that were killed during the war. 'Brothers in Arms' supports the many families whose tragic stories of brothers who got killed together still resonate to this day. Robin took me to the little city of Ypres, where every night at precisely 8am, come rain come shine, there is always someone at the 'Menin Gate Memorial to the Missing' to pay respect to the thousands that gave their life for our freedom. Can you imagine that? Every night without fail! On that freezing Tuesday night in November 2021, we stood amongst a crowd of 200. What a surprise! Where did all these people come from? We then heard the trumpets signal a moment of silence. It was riveting. But what shook my world was the encounter later that night with Johans, a seemingly 'simple' pub owner.

The pub gave out the only light in an area of many canals and road tracks that just about fit my car wheels. There were ditches on both sides, and later I came to know that this route crossed through thousands and thousands of war graveyards. I faithfully followed Robin's instructions which she confidently voiced, and we arrived in safety, as if some Chi force had swept us there. We were greeted by a generous smile and a mug of hot chocolate, heaped with cream.

Johans, the local archaeologist, as he was known in the area, described his life's passion. He made sure that every body that was exhumed whilst new roads were opened in modern Belgium was given a place in the war cemeteries and that the deceased's living family members were contacted, even as far away as Australia. His detailed descriptions of his finds may have seemed macabre if taken out of context. This is where I grasped, however, that death and life go hand in hand, and that I'm alive because of those that gave their life before me.

The new lifesize bronze statue of 'Brothers in Arms', symbolising the tragic moment at the battlefield of Westhoek of the two Australian soldiers, the Hunter brothers. John Hunter dies in younger Jim Hunter's arms.

All of them, known or unknown, regardless of country, race or religion. Those who, in their own way, gave their lives and still are giving their life every second for me to enjoy moments of hot chocolate and cream. This encounter unveiled a possible explanation as to why on both sides of my family, both Welsh and Cretan, there has always been an unspoken grief of the survivors' guilt and a mindset that 'life is a fight' for survival, only demonstrating how imprints pass on from one generation to the next, shaping our unconscious behavioural patterns.

Then and there, I decided that the least I can do is to thank the souls of the departed for this gift of life by living my own life to its fullest! This meant that I had to make sure that I do not spill a drop! Not *one* drop of life!!

There are countless more stories of my 10,000km journey within and the shifts in consciousness that I lived through. These will be the topic of my next book. Here, I was keen to give you, my dear companion, a taster of this 'hot chocolate', which is surprisingly smooth and nourishing, and so much worth the bumpy ride to get to it. The knowledge of its existence now gives me a reason to smile like the Cheshire Cat in Alice's Adventures in Wonderland.

Now, looking back on my exodus, I appreciate what it means to be a caterpillar living in a cocoon and the courage that is needed to break out of the chrysalis, unfold the wings and become a butterfly. I'm also starting to realise that speaking your truth, even telling your truth, is not enough. You need to live your truth. You need to lead by example. In your very own style, in your very own arena.

If I can do it, you surely can too! It is not a matter of how many others you lead by example, but it is a matter of how authentically you do it and how persistent you are. And I promise you, my dear, that the rewards are unexpected and unimaginable. A shift from surface-level, plastic living to deeply connecting with all that is. An unshakable inner smile, even in your darkest moments, which will inevitably still come, as this is the fabric of life.

As Lao Tzu quite simply put it: 'Returning is the motion of the Dao.'

The Day-by-Day Intentions of a Heart-Led Leader

I recently saw a crowd of people gathering by the side of an icy lake. It was just before sunset. As I move closer, I couldn't believe my eyes! A person is actually in the lake, breaking the thick ice with a stick. At first, I thought it must be someone that has gone crazy. But after a few minutes, I realised that the rhythmic movements and persistence were an act of self-sacrifice. This human being is trying to reach a teenage swan trapped in the ice in the middle of the lake. I feel we are all holding our breath. I have never seen a person with so much strength, so much focus, so much courage.

Suddenly, with one last, well-timed and decisive blow a huge chunk of ice shatters next to the swan. Without missing a beat, the teenager spreads its wings and takes off free! I approach the edge ready to see if I can do anything to help prevent this brave person from freezing to death. Calmly, without panic or pretentiousness, a beaming but visibly discoloured young lady emerges from the lake. Her eyes are sparkling. She smiles. By this time most by-standers have already left. The show is over. A lady approaches the young woman and whispers to her in awe, 'You are an angel!' Another asks whether someone could give this heroine a lift home. I immediately jump in eager to play a small role in this extraordinary, spontaneous act of compassion and I run like the wind halfway around the lake to bring the car.

Her name is Iris, just like the Greek goddess whose mission was to bring messages from the gods to the people. The young woman's mother, who was also present on the scene and previously standing white-knuckled by the water's edge, explains, 'I travelled from Kent today to pay her a visit. We came to the lake for a gentle stroll and, next moment, Iris was already diving in.' This amazing encounter is yet another reminder that becoming an example of a compassionate leader does not require a job title, nor a well drafted action plan. It can be spontaneous, during a normal working day and open to all of us.

It might be useful if, at this point, I draw out all the main threads woven into this book and leave you with a 'condensed' version of the beautiful tapestry that female Heart-led leadership is. What follows, therefore, are the thirty-one intentions that we may wish to invite into our daily life by choosing to remain on this sacred path.

In a playful, creative manner, you can focus your attention on one every morning of the coming month. Choosing your daily intention, you can ask yourself: 'What might be the small actionable steps I can take today to serve this one intention?'.

Being **Present** like the sun – you do not need to rehearse this. Remain in the NOW by simply focusing on your out-breath.

Being **Visionary** like an eagle – keep your focus on an intention that is close to your heart. Immerse yourself in the feeling that it is a reality NOW. Fly above it all and see the big picture. If you can dream it, it will happen! Care not about 'how' it will happen.

Believing like the budding almond tree in winter that you already have all the resources you need. If you think you are missing something, it will come to you exactly when you need it. Simply ask for it once and keep faith it will.

Being **a Warrior** not a soldier – become your fear's best friend. Remain in the driving seat by accepting that fear is part of being human. By not resisting it, it will start to subside. Take charge of your own life and draw strength from your centre. In this way you will command yourself well and will have the wisdom to take action only when needed.

Being **Forgiving** like Gaia – have 'heart'. See the good in everybody and free yourself and others of 'debts' and past 'hooks'. You are good, too. Guilt is so energy draining. Release yourself from unresolved hurt, then you will become resilient.

Being **Gentle** towards yourself – put your 'mask' on first before taking care of others. Take a daily stroll to your 'power place' in nature to recharge.

Being **Generous** – be willing to give more than you receive. Be of service and collaborate.

Being **the Ocean** – keep your core untouched, no matter what the circumstances. Just like the surface waves, emotions and thoughts come and go. You are consciousness itself.

Being **Wild** like a wolf – do everything as if it is the last thing you will ever get to do. So be outrageously childlike.

Being **Creative** – live enthusiastically without limits. Be 'in-spired'. Be enthused! In Greek 'ενθουσιασμός', pronounced 'enthusiasmos' literally means that 'God resides within you.'

Being **Graceful** – face challenges as if you are an enchanting swan gliding on a crystalline lake. Adapt. Sometimes practice Aikido and duck instead of attacking or defending yourself, by choosing your 'battles' well.

Being **Lean** – follow the law of least effort. 'Big doors swing on small hinges', so take baby steps, one at a time. Know and stick to your values. They are your daily compass in setting priorities.

Being **Grateful** – shift your awareness to detailed positive things that have happened in your day: events that have helped you change or make a shift. Can you write down five things you are grateful for today?

Being **Humble** – remain vulnerable. Allow your 'soft spot' to show. Admit that you do not know everything and acknowledge the worth of others. Humour yourself!

Being **a Beginner** – unlearn in order to learn.

Being **Discerning** – know when to 'let go' and when to say a strong 'NO'. Not all fights are worth fighting. Being a compassionate leader does not mean that you are always 'soft' or a 'roll-over'.

Being **Spacious** – invite in your sky all the colours of the wainbow and create community; be all-involving.

Being **in Harmony** – keep your balance at all times by remembering the universal truths. Walk on life's tightrope like a skillful trapeze artist, swiftly, elegantly and with the utmost precision.

Being **a Mother** – nurture and embrace those in need of love, including all plants and animals. Align with Mother Earth.

Being **a Sister** – the future of the world relies on co-operation. Connect and share experiences with other women. Tap into the feminine collective wisdom and the maternal lineage.

Being **Joyous** – do whatever makes your soul sing. When things get 'sticky', simply take a break and waltz!

Being **The Light** – become the lighthouse for the people that are looking for you. 'Travel light, live light, spread the light, be Light.' Yogi Bhajan.

Being **A Tree** – see what it would feel, look and sound like to be a 'champion' tree, meaning a tree that is considered to be the biggest, oldest and healthiest of its kind.

Being **The Wind** – become light and airy. Feel strong and powerful, spin around opening your arms. Try blowing the clouds away in the sky. Imagine you are caressing leaves and mountain tops. Take a few powerful lion breaths.

Being **Fluid** – become like water, flexible, finding a way around rocks. Changing forms, from lake water to mist, to cloud, to rain, to stream, to river, to sea and then back again to sea dew, to cloud etc.

Being **The Fire** – imagine the flame within you, located in the area of your chest centre. Imagine that each person you meet also has a flame burning within them. Why not become the warm, welcoming, bright centre of somebody who needs it today? Just like a fireplace on a cold, rainy night.

Being **Relaxed** – yes, simply drop all your lists for today. They will still be there tomorrow for you to do. You can afford to put your feet up for a day. If not today, when?

Being **Alternative** – try a new health promoting practice. See which of your beliefs is still stuck in the old world. Can you shift it or consider what it would be like to live by another more progressive belief?

Being **Upside Down** – bending your knees, gradually and gently lower your head towards your toes and see how the world looks like upside down. What else could you do the other way round? Maybe try writing with your less dominant hand?

Being **Playful** – become childlike. Remember the enthusiasm of a child. What is it like to taste ice cream for the very first time?

Being **Healthy** – take a health self-audit. What little step could you take today towards improving your physical health? What daily habit choices would have the best consequences for your soul's vessel, your body? And which *one* choice would you like to put into action today?

Mindfulness

Below you will find a set of questions you may find helpful to reflect upon in a space of silence from time to time. They mirror the HEART-led™ blueprint I mentioned at the start of the book.

SELF-COMPASSION

- What new aspect of myself am I fearing of bringing into my life right now?
- What is the source of this fear?
- Where do I hold it in my body?
- Are there any physical movements that help me feel better? A self-hug, for example?
  - What three, gentle actions can I take to allow it in and to experiment with it in my life?
  - How can I support myself while doing so?

SELF-EXPLORATION

- What are my three most important values, beliefs and people in my life right now?
- Am I appreciating their importance and is my life in sync with them right now? For instance, am I dedicating enough time to them in my daily life?
- If not, what ten small actions can I take to realign with them?

SELF-INFLUENCE

- What is in my control in my life right now?
- What actions or new behaviours can I adopt to let go of what is not in my capability to control?
- How do I feel about practicing 'Wu Wei', the practice of non-doing?

- What five actions can I take to refocus my attention to create adventure, aliveness and joy in my life?

SYSTEMIC AWARENESS

- Do I see this planet as a friendly place right now?
- Why? What would be five examples of its benevolence or of its harshness in my life right now?
- What patterns am I mirroring in my life right now from my external environment?
- What five lifestyle changes could I take to contribute towards my community's sustainability?

RELATIONAL INFLUENCE

- What is the pattern that I follow to cope with conflict?
- How does this pattern affect my life?
- What is the lesson here for me, and how can I support the replacement of this pattern with a more empowering one?
- Could I be more outspoken about my values and beliefs? Could I take the lead in a project or be the one to introduce a new method?
- What five actions could I take this week to spread joy and hope for others?

MINDFULNESS

- Which day of the week can I dedicate to mindful cooking and eating?
- How about trying aimless wondering once a week and observe how I feel at the end of it?
- What three hacks could I discover to make me a better listener?
- What actions can I take to introduce ten minutes of daily sitting practice?

An Open Invitation to Join Forces

The realisation of the role of self-compassion as the linchpin of compassionate leadership, mentioned in the first chapter of this book, arose from the self-leadership course I taught for seven years to final-year students in the School of Management and Economics at the Hellenic Mediterranean University in Crete, Greece. It was initially developed as an offshoot to the first-year management course and my observations, reflections and discussions as a manager, coach and teacher:

One cannot be an effective manager without being first and foremost effective at self-management. The available academic textbooks on management lack such an approach.

From an ecological viewpoint, the world desperately requires compassionate leaders, and less so *simply* 'effective' managers. Moreover, as with effective management, a prerequisite of compassionate leadership is a highly developed ability for self-leadership and self-compassion.

The majority of the young adults, especially young women, lack self-esteem, have low self-efficacy and therefore generally adopt a pessimistic view of life and their prospects. They have forgotten how to dream and see no reason to find a purpose in life. Their belief is in most cases that they are powerless. Consequently, their goal-setting skills, motivation levels and success rates are, with very few exceptions, low. This is reflected in the job market with the recent 'Big Resignation' movement that took place after the pandemic. According to a worldwide 2022 study by Gallup, less than 21 percent of employees are engaged in work. Frequent comments from employees were that 'they don't find their work meaningful, they don't think their lives are going well or don't feel hopeful about their future'.

Although employers seek to recruit 'ready to run' employees who are fully competent in interpersonal and creative, complex, problem-solving skills, the education provided from early school years to higher education lacks the teaching of *skills for life*. Studies in this area, revealed that self-compassion positively affects the development of such skills which, in turn, increases leadership effectiveness. In hindsight, my experience of the seven-year application of the Heart-led training blueprint in management education suggests that compassionate self-leadership *can* be taught, and that it can be transferred to a variety of learning contexts both in higher education and the workplace with encouraging results. You can find out more details about this in my peer-reviewed academic paper listed in the Further Reading section at the end of this book.

The role of a teacher, especially in the realm of social studies, is not only to transfer cognitive knowledge but also to instill humanitarian values, in tune with ecology, and to facilitate the development of responsible self-led adults who can become leaders in any setting.

'Be the change you wish to see in the world.'
Gandhi

I'm by now convinced that an awakening of our innate, compassionate nature can flourish through appropriate, experiential, nature-based training. In a sense, this is my intention: to continue the development of such virtues-based schooling, and work towards manifesting a 'School of Self-Leaders', an incubator, a playground where young people's eyes will *always* sparkle. I envisage that this will be the space in which young people will be allowed to develop transferrable skills, experiment and explore what are their unique talents in a supportive way, sometimes taking on the role of teacher or mentor themselves. I use the term 'space' here with a much wider meaning than geographical space and physical surroundings. Travelling and interacting with other civilisations and natural landscapes can serve as alternative settings for the school's playing field, encouraging global, active engagement.

So, this is an open invitation to all of you who are now reading this last page to join me, and so many others, across the planet doing similar work, on what promises to be a soaring journey towards the blazing Golden Sun of Compassionate Leadership, where masculine and feminine energies harmoniously connect and merge into One. Let the light of the Golden Sun stream forth and unite the hearts of young women and men alike. Let its warmth keep the flame of humanity alive and accelerate the return of an enlightened society.

May it be so. **Γένοιτο**.

And may the Force be with you.

'Done is better than perfect!'

Sheryl Sandberg, Chief Operating Officer at Facebook

'On the other side of your fear is the life that you want.'

Jack Canfield

References and Further Reading

Amma (Sri Mata Amritanandamayi Devi), (2003), *The Awakening of Universal Motherhood*, Mata Amritanandamayi Mission Trust, Kerala, India.

Bourgeault, C. (2010), *The Meaning of Mary Magdalene: Discovering the Woman at the Heart of Christianity*, Shambhala Publications, US.

Carroll, M., (2012), *Fearless at Work*, Shambhala Publications, US.

Coelho Pablo, (2014), *The Alchemist*, HarperOne.

Gallup, (2022), State of the Global Workplace 2022 Report, available at: https://www.gallup.com/workplace/349484/state-of-the-global-workplace.aspx#ite-393218 [accessed 13/11/2022]

Hopwood, M., (2019), *Mother: A Human Love Story*, Birlinn Ltd., UK.

Jowett, B. (2018), *The Republic: Translation of Plato's Republic*, Independently published.

Kazantzakis Nikos, (2012), *Report to Greko*, Simon & Schuster

Kempton, S. (2013), *Awakening Shakti : The Transformative Power of the Goddesses of Yoga*, Sounds True Inc, US.

Gimian, J. and Boyce, B., (2008), *The Rules of Victory: How to transform chaos and conflict – Strategies from the Art of War*, Shambhala Publicatioss, US.

Millman, D., (2006), *Way of the Peaceful Warrior: A Book That Changes Lives*, HJ Kramer, UK.

Reeves, C.D.C., (2014), *Nicomachean Ethics (The New Hackett Aristotle): Translation and Commentary*, Hackett Publishing Company, Inc.

Sandberg, S. (2013), *Lean In: Women, Work, and the Will to Lead*, Knopf, US.

Tzortzaki, A.M. (2022), Developing compassionate self-leadership: a conceptual framework for leadership effectiveness in the digital age, *Journal of Global Business Advancement*, vol. 15, no.3 pp. 272-296.

Tolle Eckhart, (2004), *The Power of Now*, Namaste Publishing.

Wegela, K. K., (2011), *What really helps: Using mindfulness and compassionate presence to help, support, and encourage others*, Shambhala Publications, US.

Von Foster H. and Broecker M., (2015), *Part of the World*, CreateSpace Independent Publishing Platform.

Zander, B. and Stone Zander, R., (2000), *The Art of Possibility*, Harvard Business Review Press, US.

Inspiring Website links

www.artofjoy.gr (click on the English flag on the top right of the home screen for the English version). This is my personal site and from here you can enroll to receive a free 'Note for Joy' every month, a short email reminder of how to live a more joyous life and also follow or contribute the blog. From time to time, I also organise online live gatherings of like-minded people, with no fixed agenda, allowing for whatever needs to arise organically. I call these 'e-cafes with Alexia'.

www.schooloflostborders.net
www.ancienthealingways.co.uk
www.ted.com

Useful YouTube links

On the 'Iris Art of Joy' YouTube channel, you can watch my short videos on: SOLUTIONS: Time Management and Basic Values.

'Jesus' Female Disciples' – a revealing 2018 documentary, where Theologians Dr Helen Bond and Dr Joan Taylor embark on a journey around the world in search of evidence of the role played by women in the beginnings of Christianity. Also excellent is their talk in St Paul's Cathedral (of all places!), 'My Soul Glorifies the Lord: Jesus' female disciples'.

'Yoga with Adriene' channel, a rich source of yoga practices, varied in time duration. Themes range from Yoga for Brain Power to Sunrise Yoga and Yoga for Upper Back Pain or for Courage. Explore!
'Pick up Limes' channel, with Sadia on lifestyle: healthy eating, sleeping habits, exercise, minimalism, etc.

'The School of Life' – short snippets of life with a teaching.

'Jonna Jinton'. An embodiment of a female, compassionate leader. A Swedish artist, musician and filmmaker that shows us by living her truth how to connect with nature and our inner guide. Her vlogs are always enchanting and serene.

'Green Renaissance' – a channel dedicated to filming and capturing beautiful and meaningful life stories. The messages are inspirational and soul nourishing.

'Wisdom from North', with Jannecke Øinæs. She interviews some very alternative people from all over the world. Her intention is to expand consciousness. Be warned, you need to keep a very open mind here!

'Life Explained videos' by Hans Wilhelm on the laws of the universe. An open mind is needed here too, as Hans talks about some hard-hitting facts. His sketches are beautiful though!

ACKNOWLEDGEMENTS

First and foremost, I'm deeply grateful to my parents who were, after all, my first teachers in this world and took on the, at times, unpleasant role of training me into becoming an independent woman. My father, Costas, always used to say, 'I have nothing more to offer you as inheritance but your education', and my mother, Susan, often sublimely passed on the message that, 'You know ... it *is* possible to get by on just an apple and a piece of cheese, just make sure you know how to drive and speak good English'. These two people therefore take all the credit for instilling in me the profound sense of honor to be found in being self-led.

I also owe credit to my late teacher and meditation instructor Jacqueline-Annette Miller (or Jackie-La, as we called her out of respect), for demonstrating through her words and actions the real meaning of compassionate leadership and equanimity. To Meino Zeilmaker, a student of Chögyam Trungpa Rinpoche since 1977 and a long-time teacher in the Shambhala tradition, for his tender mentorship and dignified displays of inscrutability, meekness, perkiness and outrageousness. To Pippa Bondy, who, through her guidance, helped me re-member my wild nature and connection to Mother Earth. She taught me that I can find sacredness in every little detail of life. I also owe appreciation to Monique Mavroselinos-Huguet, Georg Ivanovas, Wolf and Sarah Coleman for my introduction to the idea that we all possess basic goodness, even if it is well-hidden on times. To Pegki Christofi, who holds the Lighthouse light on, in Athens (www.faroshelp.gr), and taught me how to use prayer to allow room for the divine to take on the big challenges of my life. I thank my NLP Master Practitioner instructor Terry Elston, from NLP World (UK), who in his no-nonsense teaching fashion gave me no room for excuses, so much so that being in the NOW state® has become a life practice. I hold appreciation for all of my other teachers, who since 2009 have, inch by inch, carved and shaped my untamed spirit into what it is today.

However, my students, and my daughter Serena-Katerina, have been my most exceptional witnesses and guides to date. They keep me decent and reasonable and are my fuel and inspiration for works such as this book. So are the subscribers to my 'Notes of Joy' monthly newsletter (www.artofjoy.gr), who frequently write back to me with questions, thoughts and words of encouragement.

I also thank my dearest 'Warrior-Sisters' for cheering me on, on the days that I feel jelly-legged: Ioulia Mandalou, my mentor Jill Gorin, the three Irenes (Orfanoudaki, Drakouli and Anyfantaki), Agapi Liapaki, Ioanna Pandalaki, Alice from Wonderland, the Amazons Jenni Saukkonen, Beate Röeker and Claudia Schmitz, and of course my beloved (biological) sister, Elena Tzortzaki-Mastrakostopoulou.

My deep gratitude goes out to Jo Smith, with whom I not only share the same tribe but is also the one that always keeps a light on for me in Brighton, and was also my shepherdess in writing this book, by combing through my first manuscript and making it easier for you, the readers, to understand. She was also the bridge to Matt Hopwood, author of *Mother,* who, through his personification of the male who supports the empowerment of females, shows that this path is possible.

I thank George Kontogiannos, my ex-student, for his passionate support of the vision 'Sparkles into Young People's Eyes' and his devotion in giving life to 'Unshakable Hope' by sketching her out. I know he will be there until the very end and right at the beginning again! My homeopath, Andonis Galatis, and my first sports coach, Rigas Rigopoulos at 'Curves' gym, represent the 'generals' in my life, who are there whenever I call up on them to fearlessly protect me and care for my overall well-being. I could not have finished this book without them.

Credit and warm feelings of gratitude go out to Dr Andreas Toupadakis, for introducing me to Amrita University and for being my bridge to Amma, allowing me to live through the profound experience of being embraced by a living saint and an authentic female compassionate leader. I thank Krishnan Pillai and Dr Maneesha Ramesh, correspondingly, Program Officer and at the time, Dean at Amrita Center for International Programs at Amrita University, Kerala, India, for their enthusiastic welcoming of my work and for carrying out the first print run of this book which was used as a textbook for the workshop 'Empowering Women to become Compassionate Leaders', delivered to students and staff of their Postgraduate Social Work program.

Last but not least, I'm forever grateful to dear, sparkly-eyed Paul Baillie-Lane, who believed in me and generously offered to take Jo Smith's edits a step further. Paul used his wizardry skills and his vast experience of working alongside top publishers such as Faber & Faber and The History Press to produce a high-quality, simple and user-friendly manual that supports those brave women wanting to take a leap of faith in birthing a world embraced by compassion.

ABOUT ALEXIA

I was born on an ice-cold winter's day in the land of the Celts, in Wales, and brought up in the sun-blessed land of the Greeks, by a Cretan father and a Welsh mother, both educators. I strive for communication from the heart, enjoy finding solutions to challenges, adore nature, especially flowers, the sun and the glorious blue seas, and I confess to be an apprentice tree whisperer.

I have lived in the UK periodically for almost sixteen years, where I worked as a communications and marketing manager in a variety of market sectors, developed my own business and was fortune enough to become a mother

Through my work, I encourage young adults, many of whom are 'parents to be', to become self-reliant, self-empowered leaders. Why? Because in my world, a 'leader' is anyone who intentionally and courageously guides other people with the example of their own virtuous actions towards a vision of a better world. An authentic leader leads by example. And I believe that positive, sustainable change in society can only come if individuals follow their heart and choose to engage in activities that they are truly passionate about and that are aligned with their values. Caring about other people and the planet transforms such individuals into Custodians of the Earth and Global Active Citizens. The more of us, the better.

As I write the last lines of this book, I venture forward in my professional capacity, with the added experiences of sixteen years of teaching and guiding young people in the field of management and leadership at universities such as Cardiff Metropolitan University in the UK, the Hellenic Mediterranean University, the Hellenic Open University, Athens University of Economics and Business, all three based in Greece, and Amrita University in India.

I'm now also the creator of HEART-led™, an internationally published, pioneering, compassionate leadership training program which increases a manager's capacity to influence. Using my expertise in behavioural research and humanistic soft skills, I have chosen to redirect my energy into writing, giving talks and expanding my HR training and coaching business. My clients are open-minded companies that seek to create agile, highly intelligent and self-led teams. They are clients with whom I share the same values of establishing more inclusive, humane leadership. I offer solutions for increasing peoples' engagement, positive culture development, team-building, stress management, conflict resolution, well-being and resilience. My expertise in these areas is leveraged by my strong business acumen and customer-centric approach acquired in the earlier stages of my twenty-five-year career whilst holding managerial roles in marketing and business development in both the UK and in Greece.

As an international speaker, I offer online and live workshops to a worldwide audience, and have done so for companies such as Cisco and the International Soft Skills Academy. Some of the themes are on finding purpose and self-empowerment, the power of clear company vision and core values, AI and communication in nature, Generative AI and leadership well-being, stress-free living, work-life balance, powerful presence, career advancement, impactful communication and presentation skills, and practical mindfulness techniques.

Besides organisations, I support private clients on their journey to freeing themselves from the conditioning of the past and whatever holds them back from becoming the best version of themselves and aligning with their Higher Purpose.

I have authored four academic textbooks on management and marketing and three books on self-development, and I'm currently joyfully writing the next book in the series!

Using the island of Crete as my safe heaven and leading a more creative, boundless and joyful life, my overarching aim is to continue collaborating with like-minded people to launch the 'School for Young Leaders'. This is an experiential, global playground where young people can playfully and safely experiment and explore who they are and discover their unique talents. Insights and learnings come through a series of tailor-made, out-of-class experiences, mostly in nature. In this school, all eyes sparkle, and this reflects the title of my life's mission, to bring back the 'Sparkle in Young People's Eyes.'

Studies

I hold a Doctorate in Knowledge Management from the Hellenic Open University; an MBA from Cardiff University in Wales, UK, and a first degree in Business Administration from Athens University of Economics and Business. As an avid learner, I enjoy acquiring new skills. I'm now a practitioner of the following:

- Civil and Commercial Mediator accredited by the Ministry of Justice in Greece and Certified Mediator with ADR ODR International,
- UK Certified Neuro-Linguistic Programming (NLP) Coach and Master Practitioner (Professional Member of ANLP International CIC),

- Clinical Hypnotherapist (Member of the Association for Integrative Psychology US), and
- Certified on Open, Long-Distance Teaching and on the use of MOOC technologies, by the Hellenic Open University.

Nevertheless, my most life-changing training has been a 'Vision Quest' in Snowdonia, Wales, run by Pippa and Ancient Healing Ways Ltd. Having survived this 'rite of passage', I became fully conscious of the sacredness and magic of Mother Nature and how interconnected we all are.

Testimonials of my work can be found here: https://www.artofjoy.gr/en/testimonials/

You can get in touch with me via email to invite me to speak, do a workshop or for the purpose of discussing any 'crazy' ideas you may have or simply to connect: iris@artofjoy.gr. To serve my vision of 'Sparkles in Young People's Eyes', I founded the initiative 'Iris, Art of Joy', whose activities can be found as IRIS Art of Joy and on Facebook, Instagram and at www.artofjoy.gr –you may wish to enroll via this website to our monthly 'Notes of Joy' email newsletter that contains activities and practical tips on living a more joyous life.